In Search of a Vivid Blue

How a Diagnosis of Schizoaffective Disorder Doesn't Mean

the End of a Functional Life

By Mark R. Magnant

1

ISBN: 0692439757
ISBN 13: 9780692439753
Library of Congress Control Number: **XXXXX (If applicable)**
LCCN Imprint Name: **City and State (If applicable)**

I dedicate this book to:

My dear grandmother, for her love and eternal support;

Special thanks to:

My Mother and Father, who displayed unconditional love and

courage;

Of course I cannot forget:

My brother Lance and his wife Lori, for their love and support;

My friends Georgia and Ken, who believed in me;

My dear friend Betty, who helped me immeasurably;

My true friends Todd, Mark, John, Gary, Daniel, Tyson & his wife

Tracy, (Scott, Beverly and Dottie), Sue and Scott, may he rest in

peace;

Bonnie and Burn for teaching me about life;

****

And lastly to all the nonbelievers who allowed me to tap into

their energy and make this dream come true.

3

<u>Abbreviations Used</u>

OCD = obsessive-compulsive disorder

ADHD = attention-deficit hyperactivity disorder

PTSD = post-traumatic stress disorder

SABP = schizoaffective bipolar

Table of Contents

Prologue

"If you play with fire, you will get burned." It's a simple enough statement, but way too complex for a thirteen-year-old boy to grasp. My search for a Vivid Blue started out with a fascination with an open flame and ended in an epiphany of life's truest meanings. Along the journey, I have learned of the many things that made me a strong and caring person. From my dysfunctional childhood to my tragic event and then on to my diagnosis of chronic mental disorder, I learned that life gives us many chances. It is through the understanding of our mistakes that we can move forward with our lives. Without the love and support of the people in my life, I wouldn't have completed my search. *In Search of a Vivid Blue* is about accepting my diagnosis of schizoaffective disorder. It is about dealing with my lingering PTSD. It is also about understanding the many forms of OCD. Most importantly, my search for a Vivid Blue is about realizing my self-worth. My search for a Vivid Blue has illuminated my pain and struggles. Without embarking on this search, I would never have realized my true potential. This is my story of how I dealt with adversity. This book is intended to be a series of essays that are mostly in chronological order. Hopefully they will allow you to understand my life and the wide range of events that led me here. It is my hope that the essays will enlighten you and help you move forward too. It might be just what you need to incorporate something positive into the fabric of your life.

We are off on a new journey. The search is beginning...

I have been diagnosed with three major disorders: schizoaffective disorder, PTSD, and OCD. My primary disorder is schizoaffective, a mental condition that is characterized by disordered thoughts and abnormal emotional responses. Mostly I am paranoid. I have a fear of being watched and arrested. I always suspect my house has been entered while I am away, and I have a few other symptoms too. The OCD, or obsessive compulsive disorder, is an anxiety disorder characterized by intensive thoughts that produce uneasiness, apprehension, and worry, which make me feel driven to do things. The things I do obsessively are grind my teeth, chew my fingernails, and obsess over other people's actions and words. I collect glass and hoard other stuff. My house is full. The PTSD is post-traumatic stress disorder, a condition of persistent mental and emotional stress that occurred as a result of traumatic injury. I was burned in an explosion at too young an age, and the guilt that comes with such an event is immense. It is nothing like what our brave soldiers have gone through, but I have dealt with a lot. My event happened at thirteen, when I was too young to fully process what I had done. Yes, I did it to myself. All three disorders collide to form my own unique ailment. I didn't wake one day and magically have a diagnosis, however. I have fought the doctors, the medications, and the treatments tooth and nail until I cannot fight anymore. I must heed the warning signs.

I searched the internet on "how many people suffer from schizoaffective disorder," and this is what I got: "About **one in every one hundred people** develops bipolar 1 disorder. More women than men are given the diagnosis of schizoaffective disorder, and, as with bipolar disorder and schizophrenia, the symptoms usually start in late adolescence or early adulthood."

Schizoaffective disorder affects one in two hundred people, and it is like having both schizophrenia and a mood disorder. In my case, the mood disorder is bipolar, which, according to www.mentalhealthcare.org, is the most common.

According to the National Institute of Mental Health, .03 percent of the population suffers from schizoaffective disorder, and a National Alliance on Mental Illness factsheet states that one in four people suffer from a diagnosable mental illness each year. That translates to over 61.5 million people. One in seventeen cases is considered serious. Mental illness is the leading cause of disability in the United States, and many people suffer from more than one. Nearly half of those with any mental disorder meet the criteria for two or more disorders. I fit right in the mix as serious, even though I like to think I don't. My having multiple disorders means that isn't so.

I went to a counselor for the first time when my high school buddy Scott was murdered. That would put the date firmly in the year 1997. I thought I was going to get a little help through some rough spells. I knew I had problems, but I never thought it would be the beginning of an eighteen-year journey of denial and pills. Really I was just uneducated and coping. Initially I was diagnosed with depression, which was what I had expected. I didn't argue, because it seemed very plausible. After all, Scott was dead, and I was putting the pieces back together. That diagnosis soon changed to bipolar disorder. I quickly changed doctors. I thought they didn't know me and that I was too dynamic a person to be bipolar. The wheel goes round and round; where it stops and where it goes, nobody knows. Eh, what did I know?

The next doctor also diagnosed me with bipolar disorder. I stuck with him, even though he had to have a partner prescribe my medication. I'm not sure how I feel about doctors who cannot prescribe their own medicine. I guess that is being a little too harsh. I work on computers, but I know very little about the actual electronics. Anyway, the professional relationship didn't last. I went to another doctor, and once again I was diagnosed as bipolar. For some reason, I didn't believe any of them. I was in denial. I started to look back and think, "I just went to a doctor to get through a rough spot. How could I be bipolar?" I wanted to be with a doctor I could trust. The more I was told I was bipolar, the less I believed the diagnosis. Long story short, years later, I ended up going to the Mayo Clinic to get their opinion. I had gone to Mayo for ear problems once, and I'd heard that once a Mayo patient, always a Mayo patient. They said I was bipolar too. Okay, I was bipolar, according to Mayo. Then that changed. It was the last and final diagnosis that threw me.

The diagnosis of schizoaffective was too much to digest all at once, but I didn't have any choice. The news came all at once. The date of this little fiasco will forever be etched in my mind because it coincided with my birthday in 2011 and lasted until just past July 4. When the hospital doctors informed me of my diagnosis, I had no clue what it meant. All I heard was "schizo." I kept saying, "I don't understand." I really had just a vague understanding of schizophrenia, and of course it was totally wrong. I had been diagnosed as bipolar umpteen years prior, and accepting that was too much to handle. My real doctor was only reaffirming exactly what the hospital doctor had said. Only he used the clinical name every time. He made sure he said the whole word, schizoaffective. The hospital had mentioned it once or twice, but mostly they called it "confused thoughts." They had no doubts about my disorder, though, because they were able to monitor my behavior. My doctor proceeded to tell me that my having both paranoia and disorganized thoughts, plus being bipolar, were the primary reasons for the diagnosis. I must emphasize that the bipolar issue was never in question. It just backed up their diagnosis. I knew my journey required shifting gears, but I wasn't prepared to go into first gear.

Shifting into low gear means you have time to notice all the little things around you. I noticed them all, yet at the same time missed all the really big neon signs. There comes a time when you very abruptly accept what is going on around you. When it came to my illness, this was it. I knew I was sick, for whatever reason. In a conversation right after I got out of the hospital, my doctor explained to me that I might have a genetic predisposition to mental illness. He began by saying there was a timing of the cards with "a few more genetic variables." He also tried to explain why disorders hit at such a late stage in life, with the caveat that it was more likely those disorders were just discovered late. Still, I pretended not to understand him, nor even care what he was saying. It was a self-defense mechanism that saved me from crying. How could I cry in front of him? It wasn't going to change the outcome. It wouldn't be the first time he had seen me cry, either. If I were to argue, it would only allow him to prove his point. If I were to make any more concessions, it would shore up his case. So I didn't cry. I did what I could to handle my dignity and regroup for a time when I could at least hold my own. I was desperate for a conversation where I didn't feel like a kid being punished for something he didn't do. I was even more in need of a little understanding—not the doctor's understanding, but my own comprehension of what schizoaffective meant.

I have spent what seems a lifetime reliving that office visit. In my mind I try to understand if there was anything I could have done to save face. The answer is a resounding no. Like Custer's last stand, it was bound to happen. When it comes to mental illness, the doctor always wins, and the patient always ends up being the patient. Maybe I was fooling myself by thinking there would be another outcome, and maybe I was a fool for playing a little game in my mind. This game was my mind kicking in and saving me from the embarrassment stemming from having these disorders. It was a complete lack of ability to understand the complexity of my situation. My disorders were physical accidents. They were the culmination of all the unfortunate events in my life. I have no way of conveying how I felt when I found out about them. Step by step, over a span of years, my world crumbled. My analogy to Custer is epically accurate. I felt betrayed by my body. I stood before my doctor and realized, systematically and without warning, that all avenues of retreat were blocked. There were none but the one marked "Chronic Mental Illness Ahead."

I don't want to paint the doctor as cruel or callous, because that was not his nature. I have no reason to suspect anything but his keen eye in calling a spade a spade. All the doctor was guilty of was the backlash effect of his good nature in helping, and of trying to come to the rescue of a distraught soul. There were no outs for me. Every outcome would come under the umbrella of chronic mental illness. Somewhere in all that mess of pinnacle moments, it dawned on me I would never again be labeled normal. The most I could hope for would be "fine for now," but never again "normal." I should have realized it when they diagnosed me as bipolar, but it only came to me years later when I heard "schizo." The last chime had rung, and I was the last one to hear it.

I have no intent to raise a white flag. You see, my whole family comes from a pack of fighters, and I don't have to look very far to find inspiration. All of them have tried to overcome a major obstacle only to find their avenue of success narrowed by a noticeable margin. Most of my relatives didn't realize they were battling adversity until it was pointed out, as it was in my case. I dare say that my dear grandmother, who was born with only one full arm, knew she was twice as smart as most men. Unfortunately for her, it was in a time when women weren't supposed to have an opinion, much less smarts. I have a slight advantage over my grandmother in that my disorder is undetectable at first glance. Just looking at me, you don't immediately register an imperfection. I suspect my grandmother's advantage was a sixth sense that detected when somebody was uncomfortable because of her deformity. I also suspect she knew what to say and when to say something to give her that advantage, if it were possible.

The terms used to describe my condition are indeed my greatest ammunition for combating my disorder. Without these terms (as harsh as they may be), I do not know my battle. I plan on reverse engineering my disorder until I can no longer be a focal point for disaster, or at the very minimum can no longer be held accountable for not being proactive in my recovery. When breaking down the term "chronic mental illness," I am discussing it as a positive-minded patient with minimal access to studies and data. "Chronic" can be very remotely construed as positive because it implies a ratio of good to bad days. The number of bad days was significantly higher in the discovery stage, but that is changing because of either medication or recovery. "Chronic" might imply that the illness goes undetected for extended periods of time. In my case, I am hoping and praying that my illness goes seemingly undetected for an extended period of time, if not indefinitely.

To conquer my disorder, or to rise above it, I must fully reverse engineer the disorder. This requires looking at my disorders like they were an equation. Things like proper regulation of medication, diet, and exercise are key components. Although this fact may appear obvious, it is much more important now than ever before. Little fluctuations can cause exponential ramifications. Missing simple things like my vitamins and medications could be enough to make me unstable. I don't have to go any further to show you where instability can lead for a chronically ill person.

Every hardship survivor in my family learned to stay occupied as a means of survival. Not only can this be a financially prosperous strategy, it has other rewards as well. For me, therapeutically speaking, there is no greater benefit than having a hobby. To this day, I still love to write as a means of expression. I could write about the devastation of having multiple disorders, but instead I choose to write about ways in which I can battle the progression of my disorders. I cannot completely reverse the disorders, and I cannot undo the events that led me here, but I can make the best of the moments set before me.

At this time, I am not suffering in a hospital. I am not regretting some dumb move that made my family jump, and I am not wishing to change anything drastically. Sure, I would change many things if I could, but we all would. I wake every day and thank God for the air in my lungs, the light in my eyes, and my loving family. I have to think about my actions constantly so that I make the right decisions. I often wonder where I would be if I didn't have my loving family to guide me to the right choices.

I know my situation could allow me some room for self-pity, but not much. Most of my family would be disappointed if I played that card. Every time I think of my situation, I think of the countless people who don't deserve their situation. Besides, the worst thing that could happen to me would be to give up on myself! I look around and realize that nobody else has given up on me. The result is a positive outlook toward the future.

I know it is unfair to categorize people as uncompassionate before I give them a chance, but the temptation remains until I override my feelings with logic. I cannot assume that everybody will treat me as though he or she understands my plight. I don't want special treatment. I just want a world where I don't worry about what the other person is thinking. Alas, that is too much to ask. I have worked on this book nonstop since its inception three years ago. My search for a Vivid Blue is over eighteen years in the making. The eighteen years are composed of the time when I sought treatment. A good portion of the book is about my life and what I did before I was diagnosed with schizoaffective bipolar disorder. It is a lifetime of yearning and is about special people in my life. It is a story about endurance and perseverance. Along the way, I learned that coping is what I did before I got my diagnosis. It wasn't until I got a proper diagnosis and had the right information that I could manage the disorders. This proper diagnosis made identifying my personal stumbling blocks easier. The journey has been long, and I still have the rest of my life to travel.

My journey would not be complete if I didn't try to tackle all the issues that I face. I am referring to my OCD and a touch of PTSD, as well as the schizoaffective disorder. You see, the fire that burned me was self-inflicted, but it wasn't intentional. It was the result of a bad decision. I still had to live with the result. My OCD made it impossible to forget and forgive. Both of these ailments need to be discussed in further detail. Yes, it is a lot to absorb, and believe me, it is reason for my many quirks, but I will cover them in great detail if you stick around.

I am writing this book in the hope that you will better understand what it is like for somebody to battle a myriad of complications. More important, I am writing this book for the many people who can identify with mental illness. At times there will be situations so foreign that you might not comprehend the controlling nature of a mental disorder. I try to convey my life the way I see it. If it helps you understand what is going on, or it helps you realize that you are not the only one out there struggling, I am glad I took the time to write this. I hope this journey helps you understand a little about yourself or a loved one. If by chance you are able to catch my paranoid bipolar swings and my inconsistencies, then you must realize they are due to the nature of my disorder. The OCD will never show. Take my word for it, I rewrote this so many times, it became an obsession.

When I think about my incredible journey, I like to take special breaks from all the man-made world entails. During these breaks, I think about how wonderful it is to go outside. I stop and think, "God gave us nature to show us that we don't need to look to others to find healing and enlightenment." The Buddhists looked toward nature and not others. They were the first to be reminded that we need just earth, wind, water and fire. I think this might be the pleasure that cannot be found without taking yourself out of the city and into the world that was created by nature and not man.

Chapter 1. The Search Begins

My search for a Vivid Blue began with my grandmother. She was a tough cookie and I knew it. And I could tell that she was going to make sure that everybody knew it. She was not the type of person who minced words. She had a rich vocabulary and a quick wit, and she wouldn't hesitate to put the two to work in her favor. Her remarks lashed out and smacked you across the room. She was, to put it succinctly, an incredible lady.

Grandma was the one who initially told me of Scott's murder in December of 1996. That was the pinnacle event that started the whole medical shebang. When she learned about my diagnosis, I was still Mark to her. I would go over and play Scrabble. Nothing changed. I never knew what she thought about the upgrade to bipolar from depression (schizoaffective came years later) because she was starting to have problems of her own at the time. It was a bad time for all the family. I was dealing with the death of my best friend, and then my grandma had a stroke. Life piles on the woeful times like rich, thick blankets in the winter.

When I first heard that my grandmother had had a stroke, I didn't know what that entailed. I had no idea that there were so many types of strokes, and such a wide range of outcomes. I did what everybody does in these situations, or at least what I assume everybody does: pray. The next thing anybody would do is rush to the victim. I was no different. Strokes are terrible villains that strike without warning and hurt everybody associated with them. Our family was no different from millions of others except for one thing: this time it was personal.

When I arrived at the hospital, I entered the room not knowing what I was going to see. My imagination was running wild, and I expected to see all sorts of gadgets with beeping sounds. The images of wires and tubes were rampant in my mind. But it wasn't anything like that. Grandma was in the hospital bed and seemed to be fully coherent. Everyone told me that she was going to be fine, and she looked fine. That wasn't the truth, though. The real truth was she was going to be fine for *now*. *Now* was the family's new word. There were so many *now*s to follow that if we had counted, we might have given up the first day. *Now* was just the beginning.

Grandma was tougher then we knew. Soon she picked up right where she left off. She went about doing her normal things as if nothing had ever happened. She played card games with her friends and she volunteered her time for several Helplines. She would putter in the garden. Then one day it happened again. We were all in disarray. It appeared that things were progressing rapidly and our options were few. *Yesterday* was fast becoming our reality. I never knew how much I would miss those times until they were gone. Isn't that the way the story goes? Never worry and then *wham*! Sadness! I can say we did have a short break between the first stroke and the second. It was just enough time to get rolling again. *Now* we were holding on to our memories.

After this second stroke, our family was really scared. The small strokes that preceded (the vast many) this one were called TIAs (transient ischemic attacks), and I had no clue what that meant. They had all the signs of a full-blown disaster too. Don't get me wrong, all of them are serious, but at some point you feel like the victim will come out of it. This time, with the second stroke, the doctors said things like, "She will have some permanent damage" and "She will need..." There were much more dire consequences. People hovered over me, asking if I needed anything. They made me feel uncomfortable, as if the inevitable had already occurred. I kept thinking they didn't know how tough Grandma was and that she would show them all. Grandma had talked about being through tough times and this wasn't even close! Oh, how wrong I was. It was close, but Grandma was tough. *Now* what would we do?

I couldn't count the strokes, and neither could my family. I don't understand what the fuss was over the count. I am sure I blew it out of proportion. Just because the early ones were being classified as TIAs or ministrokes, they were still strokes. Her brain was shutting down, and I was losing my grandmother little by little. Here was a lady who'd had a sharp mind, and now it was reduced to Jell-O on good days. She'd been the head librarian for Mira Mesa in San Diego, California. Her brain was the most exercised part of her body, and yet it was one of the first things to go. It made no sense to me. How could God be so cruel? I sometimes ask him why he has such irony. We don't dare make fun of it since it always comes back to haunt us. The whys that never get answered are always the most wicked of chills. After the second stroke, the TIAs still never stopped, and they were not serious enough to put her into a nursing home, so we collectively (Grandma too) decided to put her into an assisted living community. I think that was the hardest to take. *Now* nothing would ever be right.

My family sure puts on a show, and they don't like it when I burst all the bubbles. I blew them all down like a kid with a BB gun at a carnival. When they said Grandma would like having somebody help her, I said, "They won't be nice." When they said her meals would be cooked for her, I said, "They will be cold and tasteless." When they said there would be other people, I said, "They aren't friends she chose to be with." I shot down every idea presented until Grandma told me to go home for a while.

Oh, how I cried. I can't help but think that sadness rolls around in wobble-wheeled carts for seniors. My friend John thinks it was Bette Davis who said, "Old age is no place for sissies," and my mom thinks it was Katharine Hepburn. I even heard a lady once claim it was Art Linkletter. Well, in any case, at some point, all of Hollywood steals that tragic line.

One day it finally happened: the Mount St. Helens of strokes occurred, and Grandma was really incapacitated. We had to visit her in the hospital once again, and they told us she would probably die. At a minimum, she would be in a full-care nursing home, and she would need constant attention. She started to get dementia really bad, and at times she didn't even know I was there. I knew it was getting close to the end. When you see the last stop, you're scared, and that's when you know there is not much bargaining you can do. You really don't want her suffering to go on, and you really don't want to lose her, either. Words can't express how terrible this feels. Profanity seems to fill the mind like coffee fills a cup. We put her into a full-care nursing home. *Now* all we could do was pray.

We were very unhappy with this nursing home because they were inept. We probably could have sued, but what would have been the point? My precious grandmother was dying a little bit at a time. I fought them over important details. One time, when I realized that Grandma had tried to feed herself and gotten most of the food on her lap instead of in her mouth, I became enraged. I knocked over stuff on the nurse's desk and screamed at them until I thought I would be arrested. I realized this only made more work for an understaffed nursing home. We decided to do the only thing we could do. We decided to take on the job ourselves.

Now she was home again. Thank God for hospice.

My mother worked day and night trying to keep up with all the chores. I really didn't have the ability to do my part. My grandmother was a very sick elderly woman. There is very little an untrained male can do besides laundry, food preparation, and general elder-sitting. Yes, that's my new word, "elder-sitting." I refuse to call it babysitting. Geriatric sounds so crappy. Holding onto *yesterday* was all we could do. *Now* we waited.

It was on my watch that one of the most significant things happened. It was a mind boggling experience, which ended up years later defining how I looked at the personal things in life. I was sitting in a chair across the room from Grandma's bed, enjoying the company of a friend of mine from Birmingham. My friend had been so nice to sit with me while I waited for my mother to get back from the store. All of a sudden, my grandmother kicked her left heel almost up to her ear and screamed as loud as she could. I have never seen a limber person do that, much less an elderly person. The thought of doing it myself gives me chills.

I ran to her bedside to ask whether she needed anything. She grabbed my arm and said to me, "Mark, you would love this. I see the prettiest blue." Grandma still knew I loved blue. At that point, she couldn't remember me half the time. But through all the pain, she remembered my favorite color. I ran down the hall, past my mom, who'd just gotten back. I ran down the street and as far as I could run. When I got back, they had loaded Grandma up and taken her to the hospital. I don't remember if she ever said another word to me. *Now* it was my time to forget the little details.

Grandma died on November 5 of the same year, just two months after 9-11. To me it was the loss of one of my personal heroes. She was born with only one arm in 1920, and she overcame so many things. The way she touched my life was as if she had all ten fingers. She was tough, yet she spoiled me rotten. She remembered me and I will never forget her. Somehow she remembered that I loved blue. I cannot understand how. *Now* it was over, but *now* the pain set in. What was that blue that she saw? It is something elusive, something beautiful. I call it Vivid Blue. To me it has come to represent more than just a color. Just because a loved one is gone doesn't mean they are not in your heart and mind. It is a selective memory, one that blocks out all the pain and strife, one that allows us to capture the very essence of love. My search for a Vivid Blue only started with my grandmother's reference to seeing the prettiest blue. I have often wondered how pretty the blue must have been. Every time I see a very pretty blue, I wonder, "Is this what my grandmother saw?" The thought that I might be searching for so much more never occurred to me until many years later when I realized there were others in my family who meant just as much to me as Grandma did.

    Now it is my turn to remember, and remember I do. I keep with me all the things she taught me and chuckle over the times we shared a laugh or two. There was many a story to tell, but my favorite ones are the ones that Grandma loved herself. When she told them, she would laugh lovingly. It was the same sort of laugh any grandmother makes when bragging about her grandchildren. *Now* I would give anything to hear it one more time. *Now* the title to my book is established.

Chapter 2. I Refuse to Blame My Parents

You can't blame your parents for everything; at some point you must grow up. Sadly, for way too long, I blamed my parents for their bad choices. As kids, it is our job to point them out. As I soon learned but only later comprehended, we all make bad choices. Only after I matured did I begin to realize my parents did the very best they could. I'm ashamed to admit how long it took me to realize I was fortunate. My parents did extraordinary marvels with what little scraps of hope and optimism were available. Considering where they started, I would say they did the impossible. They overcame unbelievable odds and achieved a miracle. As a child and a young man, I was relentless in calling my parents "the great naysayers." But as the years went by, I learned that I had asked for too much. I also learned they never wanted me to see an unjust world. They never wanted me to experience a world that was very tough. They did too good a job and spoiled me.

I try not to complain about my early childhood. The thought crosses my mind that everybody could complain about his or hers at some point, because it is the one time in life you never seem to do anything right, which is in stark contrast to the praise you receive for simple tasks. Older people are always talking as though they have the answer to all of life's problems, and they think everybody should listen to their advice. When we grow up, we are free to make our own mistakes, and then we can try really hard to cover them up. That last statement sounds so jaded. I wonder where I picked it up. Nevertheless, I think my parents had much worse childhoods than I, and it really isn't fair for me to say anything about mine.

My mother and her brother grew up poor in a resort town. My grandmother worked tirelessly while the children were forced to play outside, having minimal things to do. My father also grew up poor. He was the son of a potato farmer and part-time postal worker (while it lasted) in rural Wisconsin. He was the youngest of five children, and there were many obstacles to overcome. I can only guess what my parents' lives were like. They have been role models to their children, and we tell them we love them every chance we get. We make sure we say it after our conversations or talking on the phone. We make sure they know it when they drive away.

Early in my life, we didn't even think about the possibility of my having a mental illness. Mainly, the doctors I went to didn't know I had a problem. Besides, we think my schizoaffective disorder started much later in life. Anyway, my actions were labeled as normal boyish quirks. We lived in Alabama, and some irregularities were expected. When these showed up at an early age, we didn't have the insight or knowledge to know what they meant. My obsessive-compulsive nature might have been suspected, but there were too many irons in the fire to figure it out. I had my outbursts and my moments of despair, but nobody really noticed. Later in life, I would come to the realization they had a word for it, and that was "dysfunctional." Deep down, I knew I was dysfunctional, but I never labeled myself as such, or even cared. Kids at that age don't care.

The word "dysfunction" means any disturbance in functioning. Go figure. That is the simplest medical dictionary definition, according to my research. What a nebulous way of describing a person's behavior. Doctors throw the term around, and it covers so many problems. To me, they are saying I am problematic, yet bland and without charm. Of course, dysfunction is subject to personal interpretation. Either way, it's a deplorable way to describe a person. In fact, all the so-called dysfunctional people I know are anything but lacking in personality. True, they don't match society's ideal model of what a person should be like, but the fact remains, they are interesting people.

Labels, as described by one of my closest friends, are a way of defining the problem. He explained it to me in a very succinct sentence: "If you don't define the problem, such as a leaking faucet, the plumber might not fix the problem when you call him." If you told the plumber to fix the pipe, he wouldn't know if it was either a leak or a blockage. The label helps him do his job correctly.

Logically that makes sense, except when you are talking about a human being. Humans have more going on than hardware, and they need to feel important. People don't need a term like "dysfunctional" thrown in their faces. Personally, I will always have to override the feeling that I am being called a name. I often wonder if other people have the same problem with some of the terms used. It still doesn't matter. Labels, correctly used or not, hurt.

I have often wondered how my parents dealt with the information about my disorders. They absorbed it in slow, methodical waves, but at some point they must have sat back and had some pretty strange thoughts. For me to assume that they have never given it real credibility would be accusing them of being in denial. Of course, denial would be better than not being able to handle the news. By now I have come to the realization they are remarkably tough individuals with a unique ability to fall back on each other for support. They give the first impression of something a little more fragile, but with all my brother and I have put them through, they just hang there like an island in a raging ocean.

My brother and I have absolutely no one to blame for our precarious lives. Lance, my brother, is a source of strength to me. His fortitude lies within his wife, Lori, and they have been together for going on twenty years. As far as I know, he has no real issues with my parents, and if he did, he wouldn't air them with me. My resounding advice would be to handle them however you can. I will support him whatever his choice, as long as it isn't something negative about my parents' fairness, or their effort in trying. We as children have committed more fouls than should ever be allowed in the game. Maybe I am speaking mostly for myself, and Lance is certainly welcome to write a book about the lessons he's learned. If he does, he needs a chapter expressing some semblance of maturity when it comes to discussing my parents' honorable parenting skills.

I for one would have to say that my disorders have been a fiasco. It was explained to me that I may have inherited some of it, but to outright blame the people who have supported me the most would be unforgiveable. Yes, maybe DNA has a lot to do with it. Yes, we are finding out so much every day that we didn't know. But my parents couldn't help but pass along life, whatever cards were dealt. Yep, these are simplistic, lack-minded statements. I hate making those, but in this case it happens to be the only real explanation. It isn't my parents' fault I have my disorders, and I don't blame them. As a matter of fact, I love them more for accepting me, the imperfect, God-created perfection that I am.

So before I ramble myself into infinity, I will leave with the simple statement that opened the chapter: my disorders are not my parents' fault, and I hope they always know and feel that the effort and help they give me is appreciated. My father, being the wise man in many of my affairs, promised me years ago that he would pay for my medicines if I promised to take them. I made that promise, and I intend to keep it. There are some people (probably the pharmacist) who think I take advantage of my parents. Deep down, I always feel that way too. But I still take my meds. So before I make any brash statements or quick judgments, I think about how my parents feel. I truck right along because that is what they do best. I know my vision of a Vivid Blue doesn't place blame unfairly on the shoulders of the ones I love. As a result, I learn to manage the disorders better and ultimately get better results in the long run. So much more life can be lived when you don't blame others for your situations. Ownership and acceptance of life's problems are a must to be able manage your life. If it is always somebody else you're blaming, then you must be the common denominator.

Chapter 3. Expectations

I have learned that my new diagnosis, schizoaffective bipolar type disorder, is much different than my original diagnosis of being bipolar. In my case, it is an added dash of pathology. The doctors tell me that I am not so much schizophrenic as I have confused thoughts. I am afraid that something is about to happen, and that gets mixed up with the fear that people are out to do me harm. I have to draw a very fine line between the two. Basically, for whatever reason, I am paranoid. I consider it possible that my post-traumatic stress disorder drives a major portion of my fear. The fear plays out in a cause-and-effect relationship, driving my every thought. Sometimes I wake thinking I am trapped by a dichotomy of action and inaction. It is never okay to choose inaction unless it benefits me somehow. There is no way of measuring whether or not an action (or lack thereof) is beneficial in your life, either. My friend John thinks inaction isn't a word, concept, or behavior. I think you could stay in bed and not deal with anything.

My therapist used to tell me that I am better, but that I am still very sick. I have a chronic illness. The very definition sounds like there should be an operation for it. Just the other day, I was telling some neighbors that I was getting better, and they mentioned that we would do a cookout. My thoughts and silent reaction: "Maybe I will come down with a bad relapse before this happens. Who knows?" There are so many questions that need to be answered when one is diagnosed with something that sounds so terminal. I search everywhere for answers and try to match my behavior with the words written in medical documentation. I look in books until I am unsure that my diagnosis is even related to what I find. Little questions surface all the time, with few or no good explanations. Pretty soon the questions asked are more for quality of life and less for understanding the disorder. Don't get me wrong; when I do tell people—and I only tell them after I feel close to them—they usually want to know what schizoaffective means. I can only give them a brief explanation, and almost always, the answer is unsatisfying. I often wonder if they too focus on the "schizo" part of the word and just assume what they will.

Some of my biggest questions pertain to my family's adaptation to my diagnosis. Also, things haven't changed fast enough since the doctors started me on a new medicine. Ever since my diagnosis went from bipolar to SABP, my medicines have changed drastically too.

There are a few more things that my readers need to understand. My situation is complicated. Well, all mental illness issues are complicated, and it goes without saying that each case must be looked into individually. As I have said before, my main situation (SABP) is compounded by obsessive-compulsive disorder and PTSD, which cannot be fully explained to my satisfaction. Once again, all three collide to form a unique problem that I must own as my ailment for life.

I can look to doctors for help, but the real help comes from a determination to make my own life better. This determination was cultivated over the years by many mishaps and failures, which I came out of just a little stronger. I might not have felt stronger at the time, but just making it through tough times qualifies me for the next wave of hardship. No, I am not a hero or even a martyr. I don't like those two words. My failures have been monumental. Actually, I like the word epic. Somehow it fits. Also, my mishaps have caused me much embarrassment. I wish I could have made it here without feeling the overwhelming sense of despair that comes from them. I can, however, wake the next day and go on because that is what each prior failure has taught me.

I can also hope. Hope is a gift granted by God and the universe. It is a powerful thing. Hope is all we have for tomorrow, and sometimes, most of the time, it is enough to rebuild a messed-up life. I cannot say enough about the power of hope. Another thing I must clarify is that the discrimination I have experienced has been far less encompassing than the outright cruelty others have faced in the past. I like to think that most intelligent people today realize that mental disorders exist and are not something to be mocked. While at times I do feel singled out, it is probably a residual effect of my paranoia.

Most people who have compassion want somebody with a disorder to get better and get on with their lives. It is the ones who have no basis for understanding that make it hard for the rest of us. Much of the discrimination is in the workforce, and rightly so. There is no room for a less-than-perfect performance when somebody is paid to do a job. There are few managers who have the training necessary to handle people with problems. We as intelligent beings make progress every day, but in the realm of mental illness, that progress is rather slow. I choose not to tell a sob story because my slights in this world have been manageable. I acknowledge that others have more problems than I do, and therefore they have a tougher row to hoe.

The recognition of one's mental capabilities and shortcomings is impossible without seeing them through feedback from other people. Conversely, if I went by some people's reactions to schizoaffective disorders, then I would have a problem. I am very fortunate to have several friends and a few really good doctors to help me. My disorder requires me to give a certain amount of trust to loved ones and close friends. Unfortunately, I lose trust in people very quickly, and then I start doubting their actions. I don't have a keen sense of awareness about my problems, so it takes a lot of work to keep me from freaking out. My parents and my closest friends know that I need attention and help in my reasoning to keep me from suspecting that people are out to get me. This has proven to be very difficult for all of us, and we know from past situations that close monitoring is the key to dealing with it. Also, I have bounced and will continue to bounce back and forth between feeling that I need my medications and that I don't need them. There are more reasons to take my meds than not, so I follow my doctor's plan and keep my promises. I know there are plans out there to detox from everything including my meds. I always wonder if I fit the profile of a person who can live without the nightly regimen of mind-altering drugs. I don't want to take them, and I constantly worry they are unhealthy, to say the least. I often wonder if I am the only one out there who struggles with this, and then I read an article or two in which somebody did something bad, and it turns out to be a person who didn't take his meds. Then I think about my promise to my father, and ultimately decide I cannot be one of those people. I end up taking my meds.

I want to show the world that a person with a myriad of diagnoses and a plethora of pills can manage. I don't expect the whole world will understand. I don't expect the world to see anything, really, and certainly not a perfect person. I do expect the world to see a person trying to make it through a less-than-perfect situation with knowledge and wisdom provided by the people who have made it before him. I know that I will fall, and I know I will get back up again; it is the nature of the disease. When I fall, I know that I have friends to call on. I know that they expect me to get right back up. This expectation for me to succeed in life is a great gift. Without it, I would be a failure. I find that is the ending to the third essay in my quest for a Vivid Blue.

Chapter 4. My Blazing Childhood

Growing up, we lived in a typical small inner-city neighborhood. It was filled with many fun things to do, and we were free to do them all. With my neighborhood friends' parents working all the time, and my parents working and being preoccupied, we wound up doing a lot more than normal kids. Well, I say normal as though we weren't. That is weird because we didn't really know we weren't normal until we looked back years later. Anyway, we had a wooded section in one corner of the neighborhood, and a golf course in another. There were businesses in another corner and a post office in the last corner. We had it made as far as playtime went. We would go down the major highways and pick up Coke bottles to sell. We added this to our allowances, or our daily candy money, to buy whatever we wanted. I really don't have any complaints about my early childhood. My complaint is moving away from my childhood.

I think my problems came from trying to balance an ideal world with the corruption that is inherent in the world. My paranoia dictates a view of the world that holds a great portion of people either lacking in compassion or just plain cruel when it comes to mental illness. I deal with this by tapping into my gut feeling that they are the ones with another type of disorder. Is that bad of me?

My parents could not keep the lies and such away from their children, and they really didn't know how to try. Yes, I am still a little jaded. I do remember the first lie I was ever told. I shouldn't be holding onto this little mind-shaping event. Truthfully, no one should hold onto anything like that; it does no good. The one thing I can say about it is that it hurts me and no one else. Nobody else remembers or even cares—it was forty-plus years ago. But I will go ahead and tell you because it is an important part of my story, if not an important way to explain how I see life at times.

I want to begin by saying that my brother and I went to a private Baptist school. It was there that I got the foundational skills necessary to achieve better-than-average results in any endeavor. It was also where I became so jaded. The very people telling me to be good and honest were the perpetrators of one of the events that scarred me for life. Most were good people trying to do well. I am sure corruption exists everywhere, and I managed to find an example. I don't have to tell you that what you look for, you will find. In this case, I was too young and I wasn't looking anything, but I found it anyway. For years I remembered the bad experience but forgot to open my eyes to the wonderful teachers too. We did manage to have some really good times.

Everything you see on television depicting the strictness of a Baptist school is true. We had to wear black or blue pants and white shirts. Our hair couldn't touch our ears. Our hands were slapped with paddles. My brother and I were always the school's pet project. Teachers and staff seemed to work extra hard trying to make up for what they deemed bad parenting. I think my parents even had a whiff of what was going on, but they still sent us there anyway. If you asked the school staff today, you would probably hear something to the effect of "They turned out just like we expected."

I relished the minutes I had free. Really, it was the three-month summers that I loved best. We were out of school and life was good. I loved not having a chaperone to watch my every move. I admit, a keeper would have been a better way of handling two boys, but we never knew it. Do I dare say "Thank God!"?

My real problems in dealing with people started when my brother and I brought our allowance to school. I think it was on a Wednesday. Of course, the only way this account of the story makes sense is if it was a Wednesday. My mother had given both my brother and myself twenty-dollar bills. In my youth, twenty dollars was a very large amount of money. Heck, even today, a twenty is a lot of money for a young kid. The money was to be spent at an amusement park later that weekend. We always went to the Grand Ole Opry.

I don't know what Mom was thinking except that there was no way my brother could spend it before he got out of school. Wrong! My brother got carried away with his twenty-dollar bill and put it in the tithing bowl. The Baptist school took up collections whenever they could back then. I wouldn't be surprised if they'd held a special service that day just because they knew we had some money. (That's totally wrong to say, but see how jaded I am?) When I explained to the pastor that my brother intended to tithe some but not all his money (he has ADHD and I was supposed to watch him), the pastor said he was sorry, but there weren't any twenties in the tithe bowl. I protested and asked how could that be, but again he just said, "I'm sorry."

I was mad for days. I was going to a Christian school and I'd been told a lie. My brother was out all his money and I felt like it was my fault. It was my first time hearing a lie, and my parents couldn't make it right. I am sure it had something to do with the fact that my parents drove a Cadillac. (Here we go again—I'm so jaded) Mom didn't even want to protest. Her son went to school with a twenty and came home with nothing. There is nothing anybody can do to repair a child's innocence when it has been torn. Mine wasn't torn; it was snatched away from me completely. I had come to terms with the fact that Lance did it to himself. What made it worse was he got another twenty so that it would be fair. I just knew that wouldn't have happened if I had done it. Now I must confess, that was just plain sibling rivalry. As an adult I have learned to see things totally differently, but it takes work.

Where is this chapter going? Of course, I am getting to the point where I tell you about my blazing childhood. When I was very young, I set the yard on fire. It was my fault. During this youthful episode, I learned right from wrong. By the way, this is also the second time I remember somebody telling me a lie. See why I had to tell you about my first lie? Anyway, my parents were having a party, and a gentleman there was hitting on some lady. He was leaning against the wall as if to corner the lady right where he wanted her. In order to get rid of me, he tossed me a matchbook and said, "Here, kid, go play with some matches." In retrospect, I see that he thought he was cool. I remember it well.

It was probably the devil, as a lovely nurse would say to me one day. She did say he was definitely a bad spirit, and I have to agree. Well, guess what? I played with the matches. Then, after my parents spanked me for doing it, they sent me to my room. I told them exactly what had really happened. My parents confronted the gentleman who gave me the matches. They did all this with me present. This devil said he didn't give me the matches at all. The more I argued, the more Mom and Dad spanked me! The man and the lady both said I was lying. I remember pouting all way to my room. When I said he wasn't telling the truth, my parents spanked me for that too. How absurd! Again, I was mad for days.

But the fire! Oh, how the fire fascinated me! That was the real problem.

There was a little humor in it, but my parents don't see it. A neighbor came by the next day and said, "I see that Lance caught the yard on fire." You see, Lance was more than a handful. He was truly a little terror. He would climb the walls if nobody was watching. He had more than enough energy to keep both my parents busy. When it came to me, I had my share of energy too. I was instructed to watch my older brother in school. We went to the private school for many reasons. Lance had been held back, so we were in the same grade. He was too much for the teacher, and I was guilt-tripped into doing my part in controlling him. They really did a number on me. Watching my older brother was, to say the least, more than I could handle. He really did get two spankings—one at school and one at home—almost every day. I'm not making this up.

This was a time when my mom was very depressed. It was pretty apparent to all who knew our family that things were getting out of hand. My brother's antics were soon becoming chaotic screaming matches testing parents' endurance. At the time I didn't know why, but my father was shouting constantly at my mother. It was because she hoarded magazines and newspapers. My mom wanted to do so many things in life, and she could only do them through reading magazines. Later in life, I began to suspect it was because Mom was a perfectionist and things were not working. I've often wondered how a perfectionist could be a hoarder too. It does seem to be contradictory. It is because what my mother hoards isn't supposed to be out of place. Ideally, she should have enough space to store all her books, tapes, and media. My mother isn't a slob. She just can't keep up with her problem. Her disorder also completes her as a person. Having the media is her way of reaffirming what she knows. Her hoarding is one of the things my father hates, and I am sure it's what caused most of the fights.

33

My mom is a true hoarder. Even she will admit it. It wasn't until she gave up trying and couldn't get any help that she began to make compromises in areas that normal people deem wrong. Being a stay-at-home mom wasn't her dream. My mother doesn't know how to control her depression related to her hoarding, either. Even today, nobody knows how to fix it. You see, Mom was just as smart as Grandma and my dad, but she felt forced to stay home and take care of the children. In those days, that was what women did. My father, on the other hand, was going to be successful. He worked two jobs, and my brother, Lance, went to counseling. What was Mom to do? What was I to do? I compensated by playing with matches and lighters. I was really too young to start fires. It fascinated me all the same.

My mother's depression took a very big toll on my mood, and that played out on my actions. I was the one to help with the routine things around the house. My mother's depression would cause her to sleep in late and stay up all night. She would sleep well past 3:00 p.m. I would beg her to get up in the morning and make breakfast. Then one morning, since she wouldn't get up and Lance and I were hungry, I caught the kitchen on fire while making breakfast. She kept things too close to the burner and *poof*, fire! I stood petrified, just looking at the flames. I was fascinated and completely engulfed in the vision until I knew we were in danger. Then I ran down the hall to wake her. She wouldn't get up for the longest time. I pulled her arm and she kept saying, "Just a few more minutes" and "I want to sleep. I want to sleep." I tried to tell her it was urgent. She kept telling me she wanted the sleep. But the minute I said the word "fire," she seemed to just jump. She was out of bed in a flash!

From that point on, I had matches and lighters and did all sorts of little things. It was magic. I was a pyromaniac. Not a real pyromaniac, but a little fire starter. There's an INXS song called "Devil Inside," and that summed me up. I did things like secretly burning my toys. That is, when I could. I wasn't alone enough to do it all the time, but when I could, I did. I made a little fort by the ditch and sneaked off, and then I did all the things a little boy shouldn't. I learned to be smooth all the way—until I burned myself. I burned myself very badly, and I deserved it. The consequences of my actions! *My* actions! I hate saying that. I was a major catastrophe, and in the summer before eighth grade, I blew myself up. That was my first big failure. I learned a big lesson, and its effect seemed bigger than the aftermath of a bomb. My Vivid Blue was hidden behind a wall of smoke. It would seem that learning lessons was a part of my search.

Chapter 5. How to Make a Bad Decision 101

I don't have any real answers for why I liked fires. "I did" is as good an answer as any. Whenever I could, I flicked lighters and struck matches. I don't think it is that outlandish for a child to find anything that creates a fire fascinating. I think I, however, had an obsession. It might have been the first sign of OCD. Well, that and chewing my fingernails. Anyway, I remember having my own special spot by the ditch around the corner, where I had a little campfire. It wasn't even in our yard, so Mom and Dad couldn't find it. I would only go there when I was by myself. Thankfully, I wasn't by myself that often. I want to say it started out harmless, but the adult in me knows better. I would only burn a toy or two. I loved to watch the little arms melt and the plastic turn all sorts of colors. I never got caught, and it was not something that attracted some parental investigation, although if I were a parent, I would sure have wanted to know.

My father smoked cigarettes, but not around us. He never left the matches or lighters where we could get to them. I knew where he hid them, but he was smart enough to figure out if we were snooping in his stuff. He would get very upset if he caught us, so I left his stuff alone. I usually got my lighters from the girl across the street. Both her parents smoked, and I could nab a lighter from one of them. Funny thing, she was much older, and she never wanted to do the same things I did. The way I saw it, we always did what she wanted.

One of my biggest influences was a kid named Paul. He lived two houses up on the same side of the street. His parents would send him to the store to get the cigarettes, and occasionally we would smoke them to pretend we were older. Mostly we just hacked, wheezed, and pretended to be cool. It never got anywhere. Paul moved after a few years, and my infatuation with cigarettes died and thankfully never returned. I'm very grateful the behavior never returned during my pot-smoking days. I couldn't have afforded the monthly drain on the pocketbook.

I was twelve when things changed and we moved in 1977. It

was a time when the auto makers were producing shitty cars and thank God they don't build them like that anymore. If they did, we (Americans) would still be pretending—pretending they were good, and pretending that our lives were perfect. In any case, I had to find new things to occupy my time. Ironically, I didn't wander nearly as far from home. I didn't want this new life. We were out in the suburbs and there was less to do. There was a list of things that changed, and most of them were for the worse. From a parental standpoint, the list of changes was a positive one. Mom and Dad wanted us out of the city and in a nice quiet neighborhood. They built their own home and thought they'd built the perfect life. I didn't agree, but I had to go along for the ride.

For a while, my interests changed. Besides, I was getting older, and the little things didn't fascinate me. The next mini disaster was ignited with a little chemistry set in the summer before the eighth grade. Unfortunately for me, I learned quite a few pyrotechnic recipes. I learned that saltpeter was the key ingredient in gunpowder. In fact, saltpeter was the key ingredient for witch's brew, as any chemistry professor will attest. Saltpeter, sulfur, and charcoal were my downfall. I really just mixed it with Dad's black gunpowder. It is probably a good thing I "watered down" the volatility of the real gunpowder. Anyway, I believed at the time my recipe would make a show-stopping concoction. It certainly made a lot of smoke.

As an adult I learned there were many more ways of creating big bangs, but it wasn't the bang that I chased. I didn't like the explosion at first. I liked the smoke and the fire. Now, as an adult, I don't have any feelings whatsoever about either. I realize the need for safety, and I take the necessary precautions. It should also be stated that I am not overly afraid of any situation, now that enough water has passed under the bridge. I still have initial reactions though.

In order to make my little concoction, I needed to get saltpeter, and my father would have to make the purchase. My father was a very proud man, and he wanted nothing more than to go out and buy it for me. Sad but true, he didn't know I was going to use the chemicals and chemistry set to make gunpowder. I can't believe I was smart enough to know how to make gunpowder, but too dumb

37

to know better than to not make the concoction. How the heck would my dad know I was able to figure out how to make a big bang? I remember my father being so proud that he went and bought an extra-large bottle. I was so amazed that he didn't know what I was going to do with it.

He thought he was supporting me in learning about chemistry, but I took advantage of a good thing. I set out to make the largest batch of gunpowder I possibly could. In some twisted way, I was just mixing it with Dad's black gunpowder, which will make anything burn. To top this off, I was also going to adjust the ingredients to make it smoke. Not just smoke, but to smoke like hell, because I preferred less of a bang. I had a system of using a coffee can with holes poked in it to make carbon, and I thought the more carbon I used, the more it would smoke. In retrospect, my recipe didn't even have to be good. Matter of fact, mine was bad enough to save me from blowing myself up. That all paled in comparison to my attitude. I thought I was smooth. Not loud. I had to have a quiet combustion if possible. I hated noises. Noise would get me in trouble. I remember when I made the first little pipe bomb. That bothered me. I was about to make my Vivid Blue all black, with lots of smoke coming out the edges.

I needed a place to test my new concoction, and that is why I needed the local golf course. My parents' house was on the side of a hill overlooking the course, and I knew of a storm drain where I could test my concoction. The neat thing was that nobody ever used the drain or really knew it existed. My experiments did stir up a commotion, or at least I think they did. I mean, to a kid, anything like that is a big deal.

At first it was fun getting the fire department to come out to our neighborhood. In the beginning, I made smoke come out of the drainage system. The fire department came out constantly. Actually, in this case constantly means once, maybe twice. All the while, nobody could ever find the source. They couldn't figure it out because it was in the city sewer system. I would start a little fire and a bunch of smoke would come out every storm-sewer opening. One day I almost didn't crawl out in time and came close to choking on the smoke. I decided I wasn't going to do that again.

38

I should have stopped building bombs altogether, but suffocation wasn't enough to stop me. I still had way too many problems at home. My life sucked! God, I needed my grandmother. It would still be another ten years until she moved to Alabama. I will never know how many times I risked death. I know it was too numerous to count. I kept thinking I was smooth. Very smooth—till disaster!

Nobody paid attention till it was too late. To me, seeing smoke meant success! Heck, getting any reaction out of people was a success. The whole neighborhood wondered how the hell this was happening. All the time, I was too young to realize what I was really doing. I was in the seventh grade, and this must've gone on for a while. Because my parents lived up on the hill, they never even saw the smoke. They would never believe a child of their own would be at fault.

My brother, Lance, was on restriction for far lesser crimes at the time. Later, after I blew myself up, he became the bigger miscreant. I was the good kid. Smooth, you get my drift, really *smooth*. So I thought!

Lance was doing so many bad things that there was nothing but shouting and bad grades. He was diagnosed with ADHD and was overflowing with energy. Dad was working too much to watch him, and when his turn came, he was overwhelmed with what Mom had to put up with. It soon became a rule that on Saturdays, I would go with Mom and Lance would go with Dad. I have wondered about this my whole adult life. Did my mom punish my dad by sticking him with the most rebellious child? Was I such a baby that Dad didn't want me? Is this why I am gay? Nope, I was just pulling a fast one to see if you were still paying attention. It was better being with Mom, I am sure; Dad was always pissed when he got home with Lance.

I was so disappointed that I didn't get to go with Dad and Lance that I did things to get even. Once I hid a lug nut in the corner of the garage. After discovering the lug nut was missing, Dad went ballistic, yelling, "Where the hell is it?" and "It was right here!" He cussed like hell. Then I retrieved the lug nut and sweetly inquired, "Is this what you are looking for?"

I wouldn't do anything really devilish, but I would "lose" other things if it would get Dad's attention or make a commotion. While my father was working in the garage, Lance never had to hold the light because he had ADHD and would end up shining it somewhere else. I had a hard time being the youngest in the world of Dad and Lance. In any case, Lance really did get my parents' attention at the time unless I did something, and then it was very short-lived.

The worst thing I ever did was blow up Mrs. Dillinger's mailbox with Dad's black gunpowder. She stormed right up to our house and blamed Lance for it. I snuck under the deck and came up the stairs and said, "What's going on?"

Mrs. Dillinger looked at me. "Lance blew up our mailbox!"

"Lance couldn't possibly have blown up your mailbox," I said. "He's been at home the whole time." I knew it, and I wasn't lying. God, I was brazen at the time. Oh, how cocky we are at that age. Then how we have to beg when we know something is wrong and we are really scared.

She screamed, "I know he did it!" and marched back to her house. I was a little shit.

Mom said, "She's crazy. Lance has been in his room." Then ironically she repeated "I just know it."

One day Lance and I were in the garage, and I was making a large batch of gunpowder. Lance accidently set a large batch of my gunpowder on fire and stunk up the whole house. I got out really quick, and Mom and Dad blamed him for setting my gunpowder on fire. His punishment for his crime was doing yard work. He tried to blame me for it, but Lance was always the bad kid.

Lance being the "bad" kid meant he got all the attention. I was the clandestine pyromaniac. Why my parents didn't realize that I was the source of all the fires was a real mystery. I recall at least fifteen that I know they caught, and there were many more they should have suspected. There were so many repeat offenses in our house that it was unbelievable. You would have thought that rules didn't exist.

At this particular age, I was breaking all the rules. I knew better than to mess with fire. I had heard the expression "You mess with fire and you'll get burned." I just didn't pay attention to it. I may have thought I was immune to disaster. In any case, I didn't heed any warnings. I know it now. The wise little sayings are the ones that are time-tested and true. Why I needed to test them is beyond me.

I was old enough to know I was making a bomb, but not mature enough to care that I might blow myself up. I saw the destructive force on Mrs. Dillinger's mailbox but didn't make a connection between it and the possibility of my own demise. I get very scared thinking what might have happened if there had been a problem with my experiments. I want to say something, anything, to let myself off the hook. I can't. I am just plain lucky. Lucky I crawled out of that sewer system before I choked. I'm even luckier that one of my little pipe bombs didn't blow up in my hands as I was placing it in Mrs. Dillinger's mailbox. The things I still had to learn were monumental.

Learning is a part of life. If we are lucky, we get the lesson before we get the test. But I wasn't learning any lessons, and my OCD was going full throttle. I often wonder if my parents saw little signs. I was chewing my fingernails compulsively. I could have been following my father's lead; he did it too. Well, my actions finally caught up to me. Eventually all actions have repercussions, and mine came in disastrous form. I learned that you could throw all sorts of things in fires and get weird colors, or better yet, mini explosions. Well, throwing things in fires got big explosions. At the same time, I started to hang around the older neighborhood boys, and I wanted to fit in. I thought my little tricks would pave the way. I was in constant learning mode, and eventually I showed the older kids that we could do wild things. I show them these cool things in hopes they would find me cool. I was the youngest and I wanted to impress. My actions never showed how intelligent I was (I still don't think I was intelligent), and I finally got carried away and I blew myself up. My Vivid Blue would become Vivid *Blew*!

Chapter 6. All Burned Up

In the evenings after supper, most of the neighborhood boys would gather at the end of the street. It was just what we did. It was where we would go to ride our bikes, flip our skateboards, and do all the crazy antics associated with our youth. We didn't have any other place, and we really didn't need any other place. We lived at what seemed like literally the edge of civilization. To us, the end of the street was a massive forest. We were drawn to it in the way all teenagers are to mysterious play areas. It was the great unknown. When it got dark, we would build a campfire and tell stories. Our parents were overly confident that we were okay as long as we were close. They had no clue we were building fires. I don't know about the other kids' parents.

My brother and I were new to the neighborhood, and we were just beginning to make friends. We desperately needed new friends. We had changed from a private school the year prior, and fitting in was not an easy task. I think my OCD started to climb to a whole new level.

Fitting in wasn't very easy for me. I had the burden of being the youngest. I couldn't keep up with the older kids on either bikes or skateboards. I gave up trying. I adopted a very defeatist attitude right from the beginning. Adding insult to injury, the other kids had motorcycles (I didn't get mine until years later) and other expensive toys. They wouldn't share, either. Sharing wasn't a common practice among kids who were trying to one-up each other. So Lance and I did what we could to fit in. Our parents didn't make us do without, but since their childhood had been very spare, they wanted us to work for what we had. Working definitely didn't go in line with the neighborhood. Yes, it still hurts. Mom and Dad said one day we would look back and appreciate it. I don't know about appreciate, but I do understand. Maybe I'm just whining again.

It was during this time that I started to do things on my own. I got into science. My friend Chris, who lived at the bottom of the hill, showed me how to do a lot of things with his chemistry set. That was how I got into my gunpowder phase, and I promptly learned how to make gunpowder.

In retrospect, my OCD was as strong as ever, and I was still thinking I could get away with my antics. I still had a need to fit in with the neighborhood boys, but I couldn't. It wasn't as though I didn't try, and maybe I tried too hard. I remember some of the eighteen-year-olds would get me high and then chase after me. They said they were going to beat me up if they caught me. It was a game to them. I had to run like the dickens to get out of there. They never really beat me up. They just didn't want a thirteen-year-old hanging around. I guess I don't blame them, but I didn't have anywhere to go. I remember being high and very lonely. Who wants to be by themselves with a buzz? I couldn't go hang around my parents.

One day, after reading the warning on the side of a spray can, I deduced we could put it in fire and blow it up. Since I loved fires, the thought became a little obsession. Then I started to think of ways to do it. What happened next was nobody's fault but my own. I went to the end of the street when the crowd was there, and I told everybody to "watch this." I threw the can on the fire, and everybody ran like hell. Of course, we all had to see what happened. We were all curious at that point. The can blew up in magnificent flames, with a ball of fire shooting thirty feet in the air. If we had only stopped there, I wouldn't have a story to tell.

I loved watching the flames shoot up into the night sky. That would be fascinating to any thirteen-year-old boy, obviously, and I was no exception. Each spray can tossed into the fire had a unique signature and color explosion when erupting. It is really easy to think I should have known better, but the combination of thinking I was cool mixed with the sinister act made the experience fun. It wasn't just the giant explosion that captivated me, but also the bright colors. It was the kind of Hollywood stunt that is great in a controlled environment. But our backyard was not Hollywood, and it was unbridled recklessness at its best.

I wanted to see the flames and I was determined to see them. I was too headstrong, with no ability to see into the future. By the time of the accident, we (or should I say I) had already blown up at least a dozen paint cans. I could have gone on to be quite a little

43

terrorist if I hadn't had the accident. I am sure there were twenty cans on the shelf in the garage just calling my name.

On the night it happened, we were waiting on a new heavy-duty silver spray can to blow up when I got impatient. I wanted it to blow up because it was the cream of the crop as far as spray cans went. The fact that it was new was its first attribute, but it was also silver. It was rare to have silver paint back in those days. I decided to throw a rock, and that was when the resulting explosion blew back in my direction.

The flame engulfed me in a flash burn, and for a second I didn't think I was burned. When the moment was over, I laughed. I thought it was so funny. The flame was intense, and for just a split second, it was the coolest thing I had ever seen. That was until the pain set in. It stopped being funny and I started hurting. All I could do was wish for any moment before the pain. I remember everybody circling around me, saying, "Are you okay?" If somebody is asking you if you are okay, then you'd better analyze what just happened and do a system diagnostic. The pain became unbearable. I thought my skin was falling off my body.

According to my brother, immediately after the event, the older boys had to put out the fire in my hair. I know somebody said that they had to get the paint off of me, and then they could tell our parents I fell into a bonfire. I remember breaking free and running home as fast as I could. Mom told me she knew it was me from a mile away. I can only imagine the scream I must have emitted. I often wonder what my mom thought when her son showed up at her door all singed, covered in burning-hot silver paint.

There are so many things I remember about this event, but I still have no clear recollection. The bits and pieces are never going to go away. Yet I can never fully appreciate the magnitude of what happened. As a result, I know how to cringe better than anybody in my family. It comes naturally and quite effortlessly.

The trip to the hospital is permanently imprinted on my mind. It happened like in the movies. For some reason, God has chosen to relieve me of the memory of the pain that went along with that ride. The last thing I remember about the ride is getting there. I remember this lady sitting in the waiting room. I lunged at her and cried out in excruciating pain. They couldn't hold me down. I had burns all over my body. My mother says she tried to tell the guy at the hospital door not to touch me, but she couldn't get the words out. I think I hit him when he tried to grab me. It happened in a blur. I often wonder what that lady thought when I jumped out of the ambulance and screamed at her. It had to have looked like something out of a horror magazine. I was burned and my face was charred. Later I learned it was Dad who drove me because he wouldn't wait for an ambulance.

My mother said she barely caught the back loop of the shorts I was wearing. She was holding onto me like a runaway kite. I was flailing my arms and screaming frantically. The pain from the burns was more than I can fully remember. She kept saying one thing. Her only option was to hold on and pray the loop didn't break. I remember little of it. Unfortunately, I remember screaming at the lady. That poor lady must remember it too. I also remember the nurses cutting my short-sleeved shirt off me. I cried out in excruciating pain, but I don't remember the pain exactly. They had to cut the shirt off in stages because the blood had dried in some places, which they sprayed with saline. At first I thought they couldn't give me any pain medicine because it wasn't prescribed at that time for burn victims. I found out later from a nurse that they can only give so much pain medicine because otherwise your heart will stop. It wasn't enough. It felt like there was no pain medication. At least that's the way I remember it. Either way, I hurt. Then they had to scrub off the dead skin in order for me to heal. In my case, they had to get paint off. I remember begging my mother not to let them do it. All she could do was cry with me and tell me it needed to be done.

I don't know when I came out of shock. I managed to pass out or something. I don't know if you can call it sleep. It was probably due to the medication and the overall exertion. My body had just plain given out. I don't know how long I was out, but I remember coming to and looking over at my mother. When I did, a giant blister popped into my eye and they had to wash it out. I looked horrible, I am sure. I bet my mother was in shock. I don't know how mothers do it. Sitting there by your injured child, just

45

hoping and praying for things to get better, has to wear you out. The possibility of an infection setting in would have been too much for her to handle. I was burned on my face, arms, stomach, upper shoulders, and legs. I had cooked myself, but I was not burned to the point of needing skin grafts. That would have been worse. I would be okay if infection didn't set in.

They put silver oxide cream on me every four hours for however long it took for the burns to heal. I toughed it out and was lucky to only have skin discoloration as my scars. My lesson was just that, a lesson. The universe's hearty slap into the real world. I have seen and heard stories of many more cases much more severe. In most of those stories, the victims did nothing to bring about their plight. I was lucky to have done something stupid and not ended up much worse. Yet the emotional scars were there, and the realization that I had done it to myself was building every day. I never forgave myself. I wanted to fabricate all sorts of lies about what I had done, but my family was there to correct me. If any other kids asked me what happened, I had to answer, "I blew myself up." Then there were kids that were not allowed to play with me because I was a "bad kid." I probably wouldn't let my kids hang out with a kid who knew how to be so dangerous, either. Doesn't matter what the age, I wasn't cool. I was scary. Even the mothers who felt sorry for me still wanted to protect their kids from the things that I might do.

The adult in me thinks it is illogical to blame a thirteen-year-old kid for such an accident. I was hanging around eighteen-year-old kids when it happened. I admit it was solely my idea, but come on. Who was watching the children? I like to think I don't hold anything against anybody, including myself, but maybe I want to have a scapegoat. Who wouldn't? It has been a life-shaping event that has affected every decision I have made my whole life. I constantly berate myself when I make a wrong decision, just like I told myself I was stupid for what I did thirty-five years ago.

To this day, my brother is adamant about blaming me and telling me to accept fault. He is relentless about making me accept the responsibility of my actions and to quit blaming anybody else. I think he secretly blames himself. Mom said he felt horrible the whole time I was in the hospital. Still, I don't think he can appreciate how petrifying the event was. Nor is he capable of understanding how a thirteen-year-old compartmentalizes events. I have to fight him every time the subject comes up, as well as deal with bad memories of the event. I have always known that I am ultimately responsible for my actions, yet he regurgitates every last detail like it is his duty to monumentalize it in granite. Just the other day in my living room, he told me to never bring it up and to get over it. Yet I am supposed to squelch my fears when he constantly builds fierce, roaring fires in my living room fireplace. What a crock!

The day I got burned, I promptly forgot about every other problem. I started having horrible nightmares of the house catching on fire. I was never going to escape the fear of burning. I would wake either screaming or gasping from the vivid, colorful nightmares. I had other nightmares of catching on fire myself, or all sorts of other fires. I never played with matches or lighters again. I never trusted heaters, and my fascination with fire ended. My nightmares began. I am scared now when I go in the kitchen and realize that I left the oven on, or that the stove has been on for most of the day. It has been a battle for over thirty-five years, and I sometimes wonder if I have made any progress. I have had nightmares when the electric blanket got too hot. These are the worst, and I jump like my mother did when I said the word "fire" the time I caught the stove on fire while trying to prepare breakfast.

The only difference now is that I know what fire feels like. I don't want to complain too much without saying I am very grateful to be alive. I know how lucky I am. I know it could have been much worse. I cringe when I hear of people being burned. I have a greater understanding of those in our military and of PTSD. I think my PTSD doesn't compare, because I healed. The only difference is mine happened at thirteen.

The fire had major effects on my mother too. She had to watch as they scrubbed off my dead skin and then stay up many nights and spread silver oxide cream on my burns. I cried and begged the nurses to stop. Mom looked into my eyes and knew they couldn't stop. The strongest memory I have is of the burn doctor saying, "I have no sympathy for boys who blow themselves up." I used to think he was right to say it. But now, thirty-five years later, I am able to rethink his callous negativity. I can see where I adopted a negative self-image, which then had a negative impact on my life. I never learned to forgive myself. He was wrong in his delivery.

As an adult, I never brought up my burns in any conversation. It is difficult to understand how anybody could do such a thing. Weren't there warning labels right on the paint cans? There were, of course, and I saw them, but at the time it seemed like those labels were meant for other people, not me. I was afraid to talk about my accident and hear somebody say, "You idiot." I really have no explanation for what I did. The adult in me looks back and has to make a blanket statement about it, like "I was very young" or "I don't know what I was thinking." I learned that all this time, *I* was the person saying, "You idiot." I said it louder than anybody. It's time I stopped.

There were a lot of things to be thankful for, and I knew it. I could have been burned with scars worse than mental ones. I didn't do anything to my physical body that didn't heal over time. I really wish our family had known to get counseling. It would have helped. I have learned over the years that you have to talk through tragic incidents. I think I would have gone farther in life if I hadn't been telling myself I was stupid for something I did so long ago. There are so many things that have happened to me that I thought I deserved because I felt guilty over this one event. I let it govern my life, and as a result, I made my life more difficult. The older I get, the harder it is to control my thoughts. I know I would have an easier time controlling my thoughts relating to this event if I had started discussing them when it happened. Instead I began an unhealthy process of compartmentalizing and repressing bad feelings. I used everything I could against myself. Now that I think about it, I needed a lot of counseling. I didn't know I was searching for a Vivid Blue. In retrospect, the lessons I learned were immense, but I am still learning from the fires. We learn until we die. If you don't learn life's lessons, you end up in severe pain. That pain can manifest itself in many forms. For me, the pain was both physical and psychological.

Chapter 7. Out of the Fire and into the Frying Pan

After my major catastrophe, I had to be very careful in all my endeavors. The skin in the burned regions of my body was paper-thin. While my injuries were less than those in many burn incidents, they still covered a large portion of my body and were huge mental disasters for me. A significant consequence was not being able to play any sports. Actually, the traumatic event affected all aspects of my life. I didn't play with the same group of friends anymore because I was known as "the boy who blew himself up." It was a hard realization, but so true. My actions hurt physically, and now they hurt psychologically. They choked my youth, and as a result, I became a loner at school. My social crowd changed to just a few, and they weren't the "in" crowd. I couldn't tell my parents about my problems because my father was saying things like "You're lucky not to have skin grafts" and "If I hadn't been home to help you..." and "You should have known better." I tried not to give in to the ridicule of people who scoffed at my misfortune. I started to develop many weird habits that in retrospect probably stemmed from PTSD. I would wake in the middle of the night and scream. I was so worried about imminent danger that I hardly slept. I checked heaters constantly, if not redundantly. I kept thinking that if we had known what to do after the explosion, we could have raised a flag for help. I think it was a very bad time to suffer from OCD. I really have to wonder if my bipolar disorder was a major contender here as well. I just don't have the ability to be objective about any of it. I was so young and we had nothing to compare it to. At a minimum, I was depressed. I'm thinking the bipolar disorder came later in life, as did the schizoaffective. I will always wonder if people stared at me because of my burns, bandages or just the rumors that I was the "boy who blew himself up." To me, these will always remain questions. Schizoaffective was possibly a contender here but I cannot be objective.

49

I needed help with guilt as well as self-esteem. As my friend Gary said to me, "There is a fine line between guilt and regret." The question remains: Where does the line start and where does it end? I constantly felt like people were laughing at me. Even people who didn't know me were subject to my wild accusations of mockery. If somebody laughed in my presence, I perceived it as ridicule of me. I became irrational for many years after the misfortune. Only now have I learned to hold my head up when I walk into restaurants, movies, and social events. Fighting negative thoughts is a daunting task. I used to make games out of these types of events, and it helped me manage. The pretense helped me cope with the bad thought that people were staring at me. Now, thirty years later, after writing this book, I can look around and see this probably was a schizoaffective sign. Today I just need my meds to function and regulate my life. That's all. It goes without saying that life is harder for anybody with a mental disorder. I don't want to tell a sob story, but compassion is the one thing the world is deficient in, more so than understanding.

As a result of my actions and my devastating consequences, my self-esteem has been flailing for all these years. It took my writing this book to understand why I didn't like myself. I looked back at everything I did and scoffed. I made fun of my own faults and found my weakness to be laughable. I secretly knew that there was a problem, but I wanted to live in denial of almost everything. Sure, as I get older, the outer package is starting to wither, but that wasn't what was bothering me. It was the buildup of my negative thoughts. I wonder how many bad things I could have perpetrated against myself before I got smart and accepted the fact I was flawed. More than that, I was, in my mind, flawed in other ways. Here is another clincher I haven't brought up until now: I had to deal with being gay too. The combination of blowing myself up and being gay made me hate myself. My search for a Vivid Blue was uncovering lot more about my youth than I previously thought. Maybe my schizophrenic thoughts were heightened, but there were signs that people were watching, and I was conscious that I didn't have "normal" behaviors when dealing with people.

This time frame for me needed further analysis, because it was the first time I remember being depressed. Not just a kid-hating-the-move-to-a-new-house depression, either. I'm not sure I can pinpoint the manic part of the depression because it can be harder to recognize. Nevertheless, I can pinpoint the depression because I remember the John Mellencamp song "Jack and Diane" was a hit at the time. The lyrics "life goes on, long after the thrill of living is gone" were running through my head. I thought they were written for me. It was strange how I lived my life through songs. I found the depressing ones to be my favorites. My brother hated that about me—it was his pet peeve. I lived song lyrics as though they were parts of my life. It was a delusional "reality" that might not have been too far out there on the psycho spectrum, but it wasn't a normal way of looking at a song, either. My Vivid Blue was hidden behind a wall of denial all these years. I only figured it all out when I wrote this book. It is a shame that bits and pieces come to me very selectively.

In my recollections, I find my whole eighth grade year was a blur. I barely remember anything about it. I really don't even know why they passed me into high school. I can tell you I was relieved that I didn't have to play football anymore. I hated football. The coaches always wanted me on their team because of my size, but they had no use for me after the burns. Even though I felt rejected, that was the way I wanted it. I hated being over six foot and husky. I had an image problem too. My dad would say, "This is Marcus, alias Maximus." He thought he was being funny. He never meant anything by it, and I always knew it was an affectionate thing. I still hated it. I could have told him to stop, but I never stood up for myself. I still have a hard time speaking up about the things that bother me. I can manage to tell my mom, but when I mention things to my father, he considers it whining.

It was obvious that I was "the boy who blew himself up" because I had the scars to prove it. My skin was really sensitive and discolored. Even today there is a slight difference between one arm and the other, though you can't tell unless you really look. It was much worse when I was young, and I am grateful I never needed skin grafts. I remember one time I scraped my arm against a rail and peeled off some paper-thin skin. The substitute nurse (really just a mom filling in) didn't know how to put me back together. I ended up showing her how to bandage an arm without taping the skin. The nurse was grossed out enough to remember it.

It was when I entered high school that all my feelings crashed into one big ball. I had already been smoking a lot of pot just to deal with my problems, and the added stress of the different way of life was hitting hard. Sure, everybody has it rough going into high school. I'm not trying to single myself out totally. But I did have a wild assortment of "extra thoughts," and I was scared the older kids would pick on me. I had already been the target of cruel jokes by other kids, but they were in my own age group. Now I was a little fish in the world of big fish. I was not the only one to fear high school life. It wasn't irrational of me to think the bullying of eighth grade would follow me into the new school. Bullying exists at every age; it is based on maturity, and there is a world of petty, immature people out there. I kept asking myself, "How could I have been so stupid?" I thought I was being cool by showing everybody how to create the best explosion. I was paying a heavy price.

I turned inward and withdrew. I didn't take chances like other kids. I stopped acting out or doing things that would attract attention. I didn't want to be noticed by students or especially teachers. I didn't even want recognition for a good grade. I wanted out of school, and the few times I skipped classes, it brought the wrath of everybody. I couldn't have that, so I just did what I was supposed to do. I always had my homework done before the end of the school day. I never understood why people had to go home and do it. Homework was easy for me, but I never tried to do it top notch. I never thought of myself as gifted or anything like it.

I prayed the older kids would never figure out that I was "the boy who blew himself up," or that I had homosexual tendencies. I wondered if I looked gay. I knew the burn marks showed, but did any feminine qualities show too? What was I going to do when I was called a fag? Would I fight? They were already calling me and my brother gay because they could easily warp our last name to sound like an insulting term. I used to fight over that, but that was before the accident. If a fight were to erupt in high school, I would certainly have to back down. My skin would rip open; it hadn't healed like it should. It took several years to fully heal, and when it did, it was still super sensitive. It really didn't matter about any of these thoughts, though, because I soon drowned them by smoking another joint. That was how I handled everything.

Pretty soon, people forgot about my past, but I never did. I had to punish myself whenever I could. I was young and I didn't realize what I was doing to myself at the time. The truth of the matter was I hated myself. I was depressed. I was "the boy who blew himself up," and I was gay. I thought about it cyclically. This self-hatred was something that would haunt me all through life. I learned very early on to compartmentalize my feelings and to avoid dealing with them. I'm sure I wasn't aware of my self-hatred; I was probably rationalizing it as a hatred of my actions. But the bigger picture told me the conclusion. If a boy blew himself up, then he must be stupid. I am sure my OCD had a hold of me, because that was what all the pot was about. I think my mood would have been down instead of bouncing back and forth, but I can't be objective. I also didn't know what to look for. It isn't hard to isolate the depressed side of my disorder and try to see if there is some sort of pattern that fits with that time in my life. My doctor thinks the schizoaffective disorder may have started much later in my life. I am not sure if he's right. The truth is we will never know. We didn't have the foresight to ask for help. In any case, I have too many mixed feelings from that period to be able to be objective.

I wonder what my parents thought all this time. I know my dad was working all the time, and Mom was busy fighting with my brother. My actions went unnoticed. It must have coincided with the fact that I vowed to be secret about everything. My attitude was poor. I didn't communicate with my teachers. I never did anything to attract attention (my opinion was a key sign of SA). I had a world of problems, and hiding them was my primary goal.

There is no telling how my life could have turned out if I had been in counseling or on the right medications. It took most of my adult life and writing this book to come to terms with the issues resulting from burning myself. If they'd caught me living in a fantasy world, then life would have been different too. In the next chapter, you will see how being gay shaped my world. I realize there is a way of looking at your past that can either be helpful or detrimental. For many years now, I have made a blanket statement that I hated my high school years. I didn't do anything to come to terms with it. I harbored feelings that sat in my gut and never dissipated because all I did was relive them. When I started this book, I learned that I never forgave myself either for burning myself or for being gay. Vivid Blue is about both growing emotionally and forgiving.

Chapter 8. What Does Being Gay Have to Do with Anything?

It is easier to discuss my sexuality in one chapter rather than to try to explain it as part of the twisted mess jumbled with my burns and my childhood. I chose to put a simple chapter here because it is just what it is. I have used the term gay, and I chose to make my life difficult by maintaining the association with the outcome of such a decision. However, I did not choose to be gay, and the lifestyle affords me no such luxuries. Choosing to live with the label that goes with being gay is courageous, in my opinion. So, when I try to consider myself courageous, I cannot tout myself any higher than that of a multitude.

By now you are wondering about my usage of the word "label," especially after I said I hate labels. In this case, I chose the label quite specifically. It fits in with the other labels, such as bipolar, schizoaffective, OCD, and PTSD. All of this needs to be understood insofar as they directly affect the person whose life is affected by these things. You can say you understand each of these, and I am quite sure you can study up on each and come to some very compassionate and understanding conclusions, but you will always miss the mark if you haven't lived the life of the person or the loved one. The point of using the word label in my last paragraph was to imply that a label can be regarded with understanding (acceptance requires maturity), and it is to be differentiated from a brand like fag, homo, or queer.

My sexuality doesn't define my character, but at the same time, sexuality is part of my identity. It surely feels to be all of my being, but I logically dispute that in hopes of higher thought processes. I don't vote based totally on the gay agenda, but it does have a place in my decision. We've all heard the commercial that asked, "How many licks does it take to get to the center of a Tootsie Pop? The world may never know." That is how I feel about people getting to the core of their sexuality. It is also my opinion that a gay person may never know.

I debated placing this chapter here because I waited until I was twenty-eight and out of college to announce that I was gay. It was important to have my degree, and I was sure it would start a war with my father. This chapter is in the wrong chronological order if you consider when I announced I was gay. Yes, I announced it. I didn't want to hide it any longer. It was the hardest and yet the best thing I ever did. I still chuckle at the responses I got when I told my family. My brother machine-gun laughed and said, "Tell me something I don't already know," and my aunt said, "But you are so good-looking." Everybody but my brother was shocked. My mom was the only one who gave me the reaction I had hoped for. She walked across the room and hugged me and said, "That is okay, I'll always be your mother."

The real problem with my sexuality was how it intertwined with my PTSD trauma. The OCD was rearing its ugly head and starting to be just what it is, rubric. I don't know when the schizoaffective disorders started; I have clues that they were present early on and totally intertwined too. In my mind, I thought I was over the burns, but I hated my decisions. There was a residual "I must be stupid" mind game going on and I didn't know it. I thought my sexuality was a curse, and I prayed about it. I thought the Baptist teachers still had an influence on my life. In some sort of twisted sense, I thought I could pray it away. I thought gay was not okay. I thought it made me undesirable. I have a hard time writing this book and feeling desirable, but I do feel the right to exist in whatever form and with whatever imperfections. I don't think of any imperfection as being something God wouldn't want me to try to handle with minimal help. I certainly think I can help others by listening and letting them know I don't feel that being diagnosed with multiple disorders is the end of the world.

If any of this makes you uncomfortable, you can just skip to another essay. All I am going to do is reference it occasionally to highlight any points in my life that were extremely difficult. Go ahead, it won't hurt my feelings. Also, if you stay, I am not going to tell any juicy tidbits or seedy comments. I will just describe my life.

Here goes. To help somebody, you have to be on firm ground

yourself. So when you ask for help, you must be sure the person you ask can help you. Unfortunately, when it came to my sexuality, I had nobody to ask. Today, I admit I am still not on terra firma. So nobody can ask me for my advice. Still, people ask about other subjects. There is one analogy that I have used to help a dear friend who has young adult children. Her children are always asking for money and gas. It is quite the strain on her budget. I always say to her, "When your children ask for your help, do you chop off your arm and give it to them? If so, whom does it benefit?" I might be a little gross when I state that bluntly, but I am correct in my logic. If she were to leverage herself into debt, then she could no longer take care of herself, much less her children. How much can she give before she breaks the bank? That is the million-dollar question. Giving is okay, but not if it puts you in jeopardy. I am by no means an expert on the subject of children. Therefore, my thoughts are not meant to do anything but help her understand her precarious situation.

It is hard to be put in the position of giving advice. I wouldn't give it unless asked. I don't like saying "I would do such and such," when in fact I don't know what I would do in the same situation. I don't have children, so possibly I am not the one my friend should have asked unless she wanted a skewed answer. Then again, my heart is in the right place, and my answer may be more objective. I do not know what I would do in anybody else's situation as far as being gay is concerned, either, so I don't try. I also don't look to too many people for help because I don't think they have it figured out.

When it comes to my sexuality, there are a few things I must state. First and foremost, I would like to state that I am weird. All my gay and straight friends will say that I do fall on one side of the fence. I like to think I designed the fence as a sophisticated-looking rock wall. In my opinion, the wall is meant to keep everybody out. I say that because I have convinced myself that I am looking for a particular type of relationship. The relationship I am looking for might not exist. I find men attractive and very desirable. I like the attention and the companionship (maybe the security). That is all. I might be kidding myself too. I've concluded the same about women. They are intriguing. I prefer the company of women because the laughter and spontaneity comes more naturally. It is just a bag of worms for me, or as my friend John would say, a "big spaghetti bowl." Still, I have an intimacy disorder.

My first inclination I was gay came during puberty. I tried to hide my sexuality. I asked my first sexual question: "What if two boys wanted to kiss?" This was in response to my fourth grade teacher at school saying that a cute little "couple" had kissed. It was at Easter and they were younger than I. She looked at me and said sternly, "That's nasty. You don't want to do that, do you?" I will never forget it. I think it was the very reason I have a hard time being myself. I often wonder what life would be like if I had never asked that question. Can a question change the world? It surely changed mine. Funny thing, though, I must have known I was going to grow up gay.

For most of my early life, at least before junior high, I could avoid thinking about boys. We had too many things going on to distract me. I don't have bad memories of this time. I will go out on a limb and say that there were some very dysfunctional things going on at home, but it wasn't something that made me unhappy or sad. In retrospect, I did have little clues that people were watching me. In our old house, the father of the girl I played with used to watch me. In the new house, the bedroom window faced the street, and I hated that. Yet our new house was still different. As a matter of fact, most of the dysfunctionality was a pendulum swing in the opposite direction. Everything was supposed to be super perfect. My parents were building a new house. The only negative thing was shifting schools. I went from a private school to a public school. The adaptation process was a little daunting. I never felt like I was missing out on anything. I also don't have too many memories of my sexuality from these years. I did, however, always know I liked boys. The argument that this was my choice is bogus, because I couldn't control my feelings. What I could control was how I acted, and I did that very well. I was in private school, and they expected tip-top behavior. It wasn't as if I didn't know some things. I knew I was gay before I blew myself up, but I didn't pay it any attention. I didn't let myself think about it. I felt my teachers had control over me. I knew my dad would be upset too. I thought he would disown me. I couldn't handle any more attention. I already had the world coming down on me for being "the boy who blew himself up." How could I say, "Oh, by the way, I'm gay"? Thanks to my OCD, I thought about it cyclically, and my mood was down as well. Of course, I didn't even know what OCD and depression were or why this was happening. Oh, I cannot help but think it was a messed-up life.

I am gay. Writing that in a book is hard, but knowing it will be read is even harder. It isn't half as hard as questioning whether or not you are really gay in the first place, though. I did that for years. I have had relationships on both sides of the fence. Of course, I have to admit, the times I dated girls might have been the most confusing. It was much earlier in my life. The argument that I might be covering up or lying to myself can be made. Either way, I always come back and say, "I am gay." I always have a hard time saying that. I try to pin down the reasons for my hesitancy, and quite often I will blame it on whatever I can come up with at the time, but most likely my Baptist upbringing. The truth is it is just plain difficult for many reasons, including my geographical location. One thing is for certain. When I was young, I vowed to never tell anyone. I went through a very agonizing time when I thought I was cursed. I couldn't understand why people were telling me I was supposed to like girls and yet I had feelings for boys. I hoped it would change, but it didn't. As time went on, the feelings got stronger. Between never telling anybody I was burned or that I was gay, I developed quite an intimacy disorder. For me, a date never lasted long enough for me to develop feelings for the other person. I equated feelings with honesty. I was, however, promiscuous.

I think my homosexual tendencies are stronger than any self-aware feelings, except for my OCD. My doctors might argue that, but I never seem to get answers that satisfy my curiosity. At that time in my life, my OCD was getting stronger. My doctors might think my schizoaffective issues are the biggest problem facing me today. I know they consume me at times. My schizoaffective behavior has warped into new dimensions. I prayed on good days that I could just tell myself "I'm a star" like in the movies and go on. The attention is noticeable. There is an underlying "they" complex. I

59

use the word "they" as though people understand whom I am referring to. I really don't think it was as big an issue at this time in my life as it is today. Besides, we don't really know when the schizoaffective disorder started. My mood in high school would have been called just plain depressed. I'm sure it was just the OCD over the bad decision and being gay that kept me mentally drained. It wasn't until I started this book that I gave any detailed thought to it.

I don't want to say that being gay is all bad, because it isn't. It has been a challenging and uplifting experience at times. I have enjoyed the company of the diverse people who were accepting and understanding. To me, the people who are the most comfortable with my situation are the ones who have no baggage in their closet. You can tell a person's maturity level by the way he or she handles information about another person or couple. As I get older, it becomes less important to mention anything or ask anything, either. I will always wonder why the sexually stunted people always worry about somebody else's sexuality when they really need to fix their own problems.

Chapter 9. How I Handled Everything

Early on in junior high and high school, my true feelings remained something that resembled happiness in a bottle. I would set out to get as wasted as I could. I still didn't prefer drinking. Getting a bag of marijuana was worse. I didn't want to face my life. The first time I got high, I thought I was doing it to feel good. Now I know I was doing it to feel good. I can remember the very first puff did nothing for me, and I was disappointed. If only I had stopped there. Either way, eventually I ended up getting high to escape the reality of dealing with being gay. Later I did it to escape being "the boy who blew himself up," as well as having gay and most likely depression issues. I think maybe I did it because I wanted to be cool too. I wanted to fit in. My parents never had the "don't do drugs" discussion. It didn't matter; I was so terribly young. I think I would have done it anyway. In retrospect, the only way my parents could have done anything to save my brother and I from the exposure to drugs would have been to keep us in private school. Sadly, we couldn't afford the school and our new house too. Well, maybe that is unfair to my parents. They would have had to drive us all the way across town, and the new schools were the best in the city. We talked about it the other day and came to the conclusion that the neighborhood we moved into might have been the real reason.

I knew other kids in the neighborhood had been getting high, so I wasn't afraid to try pot. It was very common around my school, and you didn't have to be very old to get a joint. I was in seventh grade (maybe a tad older) when I realized the other kids were doing it. My brother thinks I got high because of him, but I take responsibility for my own actions. I think it is a copout to blame somebody else for your own mistakes in life. Neither my brother nor peer pressure were to blame.

So where am I going with this? I knew I was having major problems before the seventh grade. I hid everything behind getting high to avoid people's scorn. I was afraid that I wouldn't be liked, and I used marijuana as a crutch for finding the cool kids. Also, it was easy to blame "the high" for all my problems. I thought about all the depressing things that went with life. I never knew I was trying to cope, and if I had been diagnosed sooner, we could have started managing. That wasn't at the front of my mind because I never wanted to admit, to myself or anybody, any of my issues. Getting high was a way for me to deal with it. Obviously I didn't deal with it very well. I didn't know my bipolar, OCD, and PTSD issues were clashing with my sexuality. Who knows the real order in which I battled my plights. I was searching. There was no Vivid, but there was a lot of Blue.

There were reasons to believe my life was dysfunctional, but they weren't so pronounced as to suggest throwing the baby out with the bath water. My grades were bad, I was heavyset, my parents were screaming a lot, our bills were atrocious, and my brother and I fought. I was always on the list for the person most likely to get into trouble, but I never did. I had the complete attention of many teachers, and not for good reasons. Yet I always managed my depression, and my outbursts went unnoticed unless they were over something major. Saying I managed my depression is a little misleading, I should say I coped. I am willing to bet, the start of my bi-polar was around this time and maybe even my schizoaffective disorder. We weren't in any position to do something about it. Like I said before, I can't be objective.

I can say that school wasn't as bad for me as it might have been for other kids. School shouldn't have been bad at all, with all that my parents were providing and their efforts, but that only went so far for my issues. The depression ruled, and I couldn't see it. I was picked on for various things, and when I did ask a few girls out, they ran around screaming, "Guess who asked me out?" I am sure it was derogatory; you can tell these things. I was turned down, after all. It must have been the worst thing in the world for both of us. Discrimination takes many forms. It isn't too hard to understand how children hurt other children without any regard for the scars that will remain in the future. I have always wanted to think of myself as the average guy with the average school existence. By now you know that is not the case.

I have been told occasionally that I look "normal," and that too has always haunted me. Actually, I have heard that several times in my life. I always think to myself, "Thanks, Lord. Thank you very much." Of course, I always wonder what the people who say this think is *not* normal looking. Also, what do schizoaffective disorder and OCD look like? I will always wonder. I know I could dress the part of "gay." There is nothing wrong with that, either. But for now, I will rest assured that according to these people, "it" (schizoaffective, OCD) looks nothing like me.

I got high for nothing. Why did I smoke all that pot? If I had known a little sooner, I could have saved a fortune in drug money. I have a friend who has a little saying: "Writing is like babbling on paper, but rewriting is excruciating." I've modified this a little to say, "Rewriting is even more excruciating when you have to confront your past drug-filled, mistake-riddled life."

At fifty, I feel that I am just now reaching a time when I don't have to worry about a lot of things. My search for a Vivid Blue has taught me things about myself I never knew. Most of what went on up until now in my life has been tarnished with bad thoughts. I couldn't separate the thoughts that rushed through my head. But I am older now, and I have more control over the speed and quantity of my thoughts. The qualities of thought require much work. I wish I had control of this aspect. I always reach higher into the attic of my mind to find the old thoughts from when I was a child. There I begin to rekindle a memory of a time when everything was new. Hopefully, guilt won't be attached. Guilt was only a distraction placed on my sexuality because of a perceived notion of how I should be viewed.

There is one more thing my search for a Vivid Blue has taught me. If I had been courageous enough to live life fully from the beginning, my regrets wouldn't be so great. Live life to the fullest while you can. Tomorrow isn't promised.

In my next chapter I discuss my OCD and where I think it comes from. I don't want to analyze it too death, and it doesn't seem fair to see where it originated and know you couldn't have stopped it. I know my Vivid Blue is carrying me in directions I don't want to go, but must go there anyway.

Chapter 10. The Point of Enabling

I am going to wander slightly from the main course to explain how my OCD affects my schizoaffective behavior. So I will ask a point-blank question: At what point do you stop a fifty-year-old crime in the making? It doesn't appear to be a question we can get a direct answer. Our family's enabling behavior was a perfectly executed although haphazardly brilliant crime against every member of our family. We enable OCD behaviors, and nobody in our family is the sole perpetrator. Every individual is culpable for their own actions. Everybody is clearly at fault. All aspects of our lives have been changed, and I dare say that nobody's is for the better. Not one family member will stand on a soapbox in judgment of another lest their own actions come under scrutiny. Silently crying for help is what our family has always done best. Everybody around us knows we are magnificent enablers, and to anyone who asks, we reply, "At what point should we have changed it?" and "What would be the point of all the pain now?" The bigger question is "Whom do you go to for help, and can they really help?"

As I have touched upon in earlier chapters, my mother and I suffer from OCD. I do think I could have inherited most of it. I thought long and hard about putting certain parts of this in my book. I don't want to chalk it up to genetics and then do nothing or say nothing about it. Then again, sometimes I feel like all I can do is fight and lose. It is the same as my battle with schizoaffective disorder. I can't help but think it always wins. Why interject it into why I do some of the things I do? At least I'll try to curb it. I don't know if I can even satisfy myself with my own answers. I will begin by saying that my OCD isn't nearly as severe as my mom's. Maybe I haven't had the time or the resources. I think I should be able to stop my ill-fated behavior, but I can't. It sounds like I am blaming her, but I am not. It really is more along the lines of a justification. I guess it makes it easier to explain mine away by saying I get it naturally. I really don't know anything at all.

There are many forms of OCD, but this chapter is concerned with the fixation of collecting and cyclical thoughts. The thoughts are of paranoia and worry. While I have noticed other traits, the one that has caused most of the family problems has to do with my schizoaffective disorder. It is very difficult to manage, but sticking with the latest regimen has helped me get better control. I am the type to obsess over being watched, but I am also getting much better.

I am not exactly sure why any OCD person does whatever they do, I just know that they continue to do it, rain or shine. My mother's obsession is with media. Her OCD drives her to collect everything she can. At least that is what I have noticed. In any case, she collects books, magazines, and recorded news media, meaning anything from news programs to radio talk programs. I wish I could hide behind the veil of needing vast amounts of data as my excuse for my OCD. My mom would still tell you it is a curse.

For me, it didn't start out that way. Mom' hoarding started with the very common behavior of washing her hands too much. She went well beyond overdoing it. Her hands would crack and bleed, and then she would slather Jergens lotion repeatedly like it was going to do anything but ruin whatever she touched. She called out excessively for everybody to wash their hands if they even breathed on them. It graduated from there to many other forms of OCD until the latest and most prevalent hoarding of media.

What I am leaving out is how it affected her (I hated being told that). She is the one who rearranges her life for her obsession. It is easy to write a book and say that somebody who lives in the wake of a hoarder is totally put upon. It is even easier to look for sympathy or find ways to defend your actions when somebody accuses you of being an enabler. Believe me, I have heard it all. I even heard somebody once say I needed to find something "original" to write. You would be surprised at who said it and at its encompassing nature.

There is nothing original about hoarders. Then again, if it weren't original, they would have better rates of successful treatments. Oh, did that sound jaded? Well, I don't really mean it to be, I just think it is a stab in the dark right now, and our attempts at helping my mother only showed her how smart she was at using her enablers.

In my youth, I would constantly think her problem was my

problem. I was very young when it started, so it did affect me. I adopted her quirky little behaviors and internalized them as problems in my life. Sure, as I got older, I had the same insecurities that any young adult does, but I added to that the hoarding and the other things that go along for the ride. I didn't know to look deep within and spot some of that rubbing off in either adopted or hereditary behaviors. Either way, it is there. I now know what "controlling" means.

My collecting or OCD is more like a hobby gone insane. Now that my medicines are working, it is better managed. The reasons I do what I do still lie in a world that defies explanation. My doctors are good. They have managed to control some of it, like stopping me from biting my fingernails. I wish they could make 100 percent progress with my paranoia, but that appears to be impossible. I do get periods of relief, but only after I put forth a stream of logical thoughts. I almost always think of the watchers, and then I logically think there is nobody in real life that would be so cruel, heartless, or just plain nasty enough to play with somebody mentally. It gets me through the bad times. My thought process ends up at "I will laugh at them forever for wasting their time."

To understand some of my behaviors, I have to understand my OCD. I tend to have two types of obsessive thoughts. I've identified one type as "worry," which comes from my father's side of the family. Dad said his mother worried all the time. I worry about the future and things like death or paying the bills. I think that is normal. Type two, which isn't normal, is the feeling of being watched or thinking a government official will arrest me. I am obsessed by both kinds of thoughts. They drive me to do things like check and see if the alarm is on and the doors are locked. I also repeatedly look out my window (actually, with meds, I stopped that). As a side note, I also have a compulsion to check the electrical appliances to see if they are off. This is a result of my burns. None of this is normal. One time I taped the window shut with aluminum foil. I feared being watched. I did things like give all my CDs to my brother because I no longer had receipts for them. My thoughts and actions were disrupting normal life.

The other compulsive behaviors come from my mother. I

collect Depression-era glass, and I can stare at it for an hour if I let myself. I gravitate toward two patterns in either clear crystal or light blue. In this respect, my mother and I are the same—she loves my glass too. I also collect other stuff under the umbrella or classification of "antique." To some it might be junk. You know, one man's junk is another man's hoarded old stuff. I never let it go once it enters my home. Well, that's not entirely true, but the glass doesn't go. I have lots of that.

Most of my family members don't even try to understand what I am doing at any given time. They put up with what I do and pretend not to notice. They do the same for my mother. They watch her hurry past with a book in her arm or headphones on, saying, "I will be back in a minute; I have to start a recording." They don't even pay attention unless it interferes with an event they have planned. They watch my mom multitask and think that she is never going to have enough time to listen to all that she has recorded. I laugh when my father says, "I let her do what she wants." The one thing I know about my mom is that she will do what she wants. My parents were a match made in heaven. Their love for each other has been enough to see them through each other's faults. They have been together for over fifty-three years.

Mom and I are a lot closer than I let on. I wonder if my brother is the only one to see it. I know how she feels when my father says, "Hurry up. We're going to be late." I have to take Dad's side a small percentage of the time. We are running late by the time Mom gets ready. I don't know how she can stay so optimistic when everybody is chewing on her. She is an incredible work of art. I will never know how she remembers to record all the shows and the times. I know that there have to be mistakes in her timing, but she can't complain to anybody because everybody will say, "What's one tape in a million?"

It is okay to have a quirk or two. I have more than half a dozen. I am not going to share most of them because they don't pertain to this story. I bring them up only to express to my readers that quirks complete people. It makes them human. Our pets entertain us when they do something weird or a little strange. So why can't we take the same attitude about the quirks of our fellow humans? People need to feel accepted. People who have OCD or any disorder need acceptance too.

The first sign of my OCD started when I was nine or ten. The reality might be it was around even earlier. I used to chew my fingernails. It started as a great tribute to my father. It might not be fair to say, but I think my dad showed me how. I took over from there. My teachers and my parents tried to stop me by painting awful-tasting stuff on my fingers. It was made specifically to deter kids who were nail biters. It couldn't have been healthy—the stuff was probably mixed with DDT. It never worked, and eventually they were the ones who stopped a behavior. My Baptist teachers were pretty hard-nosed. When they wanted something, they would stop at nothing to achieve it. I can't believe they gave up so easily. I must have really been a nail biter. They gave up and I continued to bite my nails until my midforties. I cannot identify the actual medicine that worked, it just did.

After the paint can incident, I chewed my nails until they bled. The problem was I added the compulsive behavior of checking everything and the obsessive mental thoughts of guilt and regret. Like I said earlier, my friend Gary pointed out before that "there is a fine line between guilt and regret." I had nightmares that would wake me, and then I would lie there and just think about my mistakes. I kept going over the accident in various ways. The one obsessive thought that comes to mind was of me laughing when I was engulfed in flames. I remember laughing until the pain set in. Oh, how that bothered me. It played out like a little horror film in my head. I was burned and had no concept of how much pain was going to come. I would also think about what my life would be like if I had never pulled that "stupid" stunt. Oh yes, I repeated the word "stupid" more than anything. The boy who blew himself up was repeatedly calling himself stupid. Why wouldn't he? Everybody who knew was either asking why or saying, "Didn't you know better?" It didn't go away fast enough to be a simple "little lesson."

I did make it past the burns, but not the OCD. Life progressed, but not very fast, and I was starting to listen to all the depressing songs. My brother even called me out on it. He couldn't understand why I was depressed, and I couldn't understand why he was always fighting with Mom. I would do some really weird things. In my pass through the kitchen to make sure the appliances were off, I would move everything from one counter to the next, because Mom would say, "Where is it?" I would get the dog all riled up just when Mom stopped fighting and wanted a break. I perpetuated a hell in our house. Lance was stealing change from my room, and I was obsessed about that too. I was going to make everybody pay. It is sad when a person or a group of people gets together and makes up their own rules to which they hold everybody accountable but themselves.

I really was good in overall quality, but I was the last person in our house to get any attention unless I did something to get it. I still want attention, but in the same way—not directly. That is why I think I feed my schizoaffective disorder. Secretly I want to be the star, but not in the real limelight. I feed on the attention people give me, but I don't want overt recognition. I didn't want everybody focusing on me because it brought back feelings of being "the boy who blew himself up." I just had so many emotional problems and no way of getting any relief. I hated my decisions, and I always called myself stupid. I obsessively thought negatively and couldn't see the future.

Today things are different. I go to counseling and work on my problems. I don't take it for granted that my life will magically turn out the way I want. It is all part of my search. When I go for counseling, I work on more than just my OCD. We graze the subject every time. My therapist asks me if I have relapsed into collecting or thinking my obsessed thoughts. I am the happiest when I can say I cleaned a room or my meds are working better. I don't worry about being arrested, because I am not doing anything wrong. I like to think the search for a Vivid Blue is taking a new turn now that my medications are working better. I don't chew my fingernails anymore, and that was my marathon compulsion. How on earth my doctors did that, I will never know. As for my paranoia, it is better. I hate saying negative things, but it will never be a 100 percent cure. My mind works too fast in negative directions. So when the paranoia hits, I logically run through a series of self-checks. I put myself back on track shortly after. I am quite sure that this part of my search for the Vivid Blue is one of the hardest. Nobody likes to think it isn't going to change. At least I don't chew my fingernails.

Chapter 11. When Bad Things Happen...

For me, it might have felt like the end of the world when my car wasn't working, but to you (and the way I write it) it seems trivial. So here goes...

I was in denial of my bipolar swings until my midthirties. Actually, I was thirty-two when I first went to a doctor—my friend had been murdered and I needed help dealing with it. Very shortly after that, they informed me that I was bipolar. Then in my late forties, they diagnosed me with schizoaffective disorder. By now you know (probably from other sources besides me) that schizoaffective bipolar and bipolar disorder mimic each other closely as far as mood swings. Actually, I don't have to say it, but schizoaffective disorder means you have depression or bipolar disorder with the added confused thoughts or the pathology. Mental illness gains traction and becomes a destructive animal when you are not cognizant of it. I wasn't cognizant for years, apparently. In fact, at times I felt and still feel quite normal—so normal, I wonder if it isn't other people who have the problem. I guess that is the nature of my disorder. It probably has a lot to do with how well the medicines are working. Still, I am sure there is a degree to which others have a problem with my schizoaffective behavior. Some people cannot process the knowledge given them without it changing them in some manner. Then there are the ones who use the info wrongly. We won't discuss these people, for they have a disorder uniquely their own.

I'm not entirely without clues. I do know there are things I do that nobody else does. I don't like sharing these little revelations, because they are little balls of embarrassment to me. I don't think they will ever stop. The most I can hope for is to hide them for extended lengths of time. I wonder all the time why I am suffering my weird thoughts of paranoia and doing these weird things as a result. In later chapters, I will touch my real problems, and you will understand my disorder completely.

I have to ask myself if I had any culpability in creating my situation. There is a school of thought that believes self-medication plays a key part in mental illness. I am a little embarrassed to admit to my readers that I smoked quite a bit of pot in my younger days. I truly hope it never comes across as bragging. In my case, I believe I had way too many problems at such an early age that it was easier for me to find an escape than to deal with my life. Sure, I can blame my drug use on everything from my burns to bad attitude and maybe even easy access, but nothing can be said for the years when I wasted my life doing the unmentionable. I had a problem, and I never saw it for what it was: a rabid monster that snuck in as a charming little pet, one I thought I could pet and train.

I like to think my ways of dealing with my problems work for me. But they don't and they didn't. The strategies I have now could always stand some improvement. The question then becomes how one finds or where one goes to find the improvements that will be beneficial to one's life. I always look to people who have led extraordinary lives, like the late Nelson Mandela. It has been said that imitation is the highest form of flattery, but it is really a selfish thing, though in a good way. Nobody has to reinvent the wheel. My real source of inspiration was my grandmother. She shaped my life like nobody else ever could. She overcame so many things by having only one arm and still functioning normally. She was quick-witted and had a business sense about her. I could use a dose of her "inspiration" right now.

I remember one time when I was in San Diego (I think it was San Diego), and we were in the hardware store getting some things to fix up her house. She always did whatever repairs she could herself. We made it to the cashier, and my grandmother had the items already calculated in her head. She even had the tax calculated to the penny. When the clerk rang up the items, she got it wrong, and Grandma told her. The clerk then rang them up again and came up with the figure Grandma had said. This didn't satisfy the clerk, so she rang them up a third time to be sure. Finally she came to the same price Grandma had stated. Grandma just laughed. I knew she was thinking, "Take care of the pennies and the dollars will take care of themselves." Grandma was quite the character. She was so smart. I still wonder why she made such a big deal over the few pennies, but it does prove my point: the smallest of things do matter.

My grandmother came to Alabama in the late 1980s. During that time, she drove a Honda. In admiration, I ended up driving a Honda for over twenty years. By the time I finished writing this book, I swapped to another brand, but that is another story. In any case, I drove Hondas because Hondas were dependable. Cars today are so good that it really is just personal choice. When my grandmother started driving, it wasn't that way. I loved to listen to her stories of how long it had been since she started driving. She bragged about driving stick shift. My grandmother's deformity meant she had to hold the steering wheel with her right arm, which was a nub, and reach over with her good left arm and shift gears. I often wondered if she could even have driven my pickup truck. I couldn't imagine how she did it, but she managed. Later I would learn that "manage" was a word she used every day, like using water or electricity. Managing was no small task.

Managing was also the main course in my family. We struggled through many obstacles without knowing they were really there. I don't want to say we were blind to any psychological problems that existed, but it is true we were barely coping. We had major problems, and every family member was keen to enable each other's problems. It was almost a game of "I will let you do this if I can do that." We learned from each other how to tread lightly and not to step on each other's toes.

By my late teens and early twenties, I was not the type of person to throw all caution to the wind. My experience with fires left me overly cautious, and yet there were still things I needed to learn. My OCD tendencies weren't giving me any breaks, and I never knew I was floating in and out of mood swings. To this day I think my mood swings must have been longer than my rapid-cycling swings of today. For the most part, and for long periods of time, I had a good amount of optimism. Sure, I felt that life would be better if I moved out of my parents' house. But that is what any youngster wants, and I was no exception. Ignorance is bliss, as they say.

It is just plain easy to say, "Bad things happen in life and you have to accept it." But I've never liked simple little lack-minded statements. While it is true, it doesn't make it an easy lesson. It is something that can take years to fully understand. You my never fully come to grips with it. Over time the pain of the event goes, but the memories stay with you like a remembered book. Being reminded of it is a nightmare in itself. In a sense, you pull the book off the shelf and relive it. You can relive it over and over until it warps your ability to act normal in certain situations. I have several such events (besides my burns) that have shaped my life. I work very hard at not letting these events dominate the present, yet dominate they do. They have hold of me and shape every decision I make until I wonder if I am making a decision based on hard facts, whims, or just plain fears. I don't like analyzing my decisions, but I feel it helps me manage my life in ways that comfort me. I need security too. My schizoaffective disorder robs me of security, and mapping out a future is a way of saying the disorder is under control. My future is in my hands, and I am glad to know I can control things like my finances, my house, and even my healthcare. There were times I had no control, and they were the worst. To add salt to that wound, I was truly blind to it and it festered.

One such event that left a very bad taste in my mouth was when I acquired a burnt-orange Yamaha RD-350 from a guy named Bruce. I was in my late teens, maybe just a tad older. I never registered the bike. I had a sneaking suspicion the bike was stolen, and I remember thinking that the guy selling me the bike was probably a gangster. He dated a friend of mine's sister and lived in a trailer across town, but that doesn't really pertain to the story. Surely he had to live up to his name somehow. The bike had a racing faring and expansion chambers. I never really understood the real concept of expansion chambers, but they made the bike fast. I relished saying the words more than anything. I could almost pop a wheelie all the way out the driveway. What a death machine.

I loved my motorcycle until I wrecked it, and after that, I didn't ride much at all. As a matter of fact, I eventually sold it to my brother, who in turn sold it to an old classmate named Andrew. I don't have to have to explain the details to make you understand the severity of my accident. The lady who caused the accident looked right at me and then pulled out in front of me. I could have sworn we made eye contact. She swore that she never even saw me. The motorcycle accident dimpled my helmet, and I never was checked out for it. I know I flipped over the car for some distance, and I never went to the hospital. I was a rough-and-tumble kid. My brother and I always fought and we destroyed furniture. "You know how that is with boys," remarked my father. I wasn't injured, but my feather-down jacket was so ripped, I looked like Chicken Man. I learned later that not being seen by other drivers was the most common cause of motorcycle accidents. The accident didn't leave any physical injuries, and the only emotional injury was a great sense of caution that anybody could profit from. This caution was a commodity that any teen should have. Later, wrecking my motorcycle became ammunition for me to get my mother's car. Really, I used it as a reason to extort her for it. All I had to say was "I will just use my bike" and the car was mine, especially on a rainy day. I loved her car and would have found any excuse to borrow it.

My first and only real car crash was a completely different experience. It was probably the first time I ever realized time could stand still. It was also the first time I realized that I didn't think properly when I was in bad situations. I had some sort of mental inability to process data clearly when I knew something was wrong. I believe this had something to do with my undiagnosed PTSD. I went for years thinking I had made it through the fire, only to realize years later that the fire was still controlling me. This is the point I was referring to earlier when I said I let my decisions be ruled by fear. I know PTSD is in itself a battle that most injured people have to struggle with on a continual basis. I still have thoughts of this accident. I was trapped in a car that wrapped around me. It was a single-car accident, and it almost killed me. I rolled my Volkswagen bug, and I couldn't tell you how many times. I rolled it oblong, bumper to bumper, at least four times. I was traveling at about fifty miles per hour. The gentleman behind me said he had never seen anything like it. I flipped up off the curb and into a field. My VW bug crumpled like a ball of aluminum foil. My father and I argue to this very day about what really happened. He made his assessment by sheer deduction of the facts, and by talking to the gentleman who was following me. Dad heard about the accident on his CB radio and came down to see if it was me.

When the ambulance driver got there, he was instructing a young intern. He kept saying, "He might be in shock" and all sorts of stuff. I kept saying, "Get me out here." I often wonder if angels hold us in a bubble. I surely believe that some force of nature or God himself kept me from harm that day. I walked away with bruises everywhere. Not a bone was broken, but I wondered about fractures in my shoulders, which seemed to hurt a lot. Where my legs were pinned, I certainly hurt too. But heaven smiled on me, and I told everybody who loved me that I wasn't the only one who experienced a miracle that day. I will use my own words: "I don't think I am supposed to be alive." Then again, maybe the reverse is true. Maybe I *am* supposed to be alive.

My parents had no idea about my schizoaffective problems when they decided to let me get my driver's license. In retrospect, it was just easier for them to let us do the driving than to cart us around and subsequently wait for us. I don't think they would have reached that decision so easily if they'd known I had the disorders. Well, that isn't exactly a truthful statement. I didn't really show any signs of being very unstable, and we don't know when the disorders emerged. From my limited point of view, back in the 1980s, there weren't mental problems; there were bad people. If you needed to get help, you kept it quiet. The social stigma was widespread, and in Alabama, it had repercussions. My parents were taking a lot of heat because my brother had ADHD, and there were some people who thought it was just plain bad parenting. I was still highly functioning. I'm not at all stating that people with schizoaffective disorder shouldn't drive, I just wonder if I should have at age sixteen. Still, I took care of my mother's car when I started driving, and it remained intact until my graduation, when Dad bought me my own car. This wasn't the car I wrecked, and I was a bit older than eighteen. As a matter of fact, I hadn't yet sold my first car when I bought my VW, so in my mind I went backward when I had to drive the old clunker again.

I wanted to believe that there was some culpability in everything I did, but that can't be the case. Every person suffering from mental illness goes through events that are out of his or her control. They are little or big accidents, if you will. In my case, my mental issues caused longer-lasting repercussions down the road, and my ability to understand why things happened began to get compromised. Many years went by before I realized I don't think right in these types of situations. I think my PTSD and schizoaffective disorder are the cause.

A lot of questions come to mind. Maybe it's true that the motorcycle incident and my car accident could not have been prevented. It is sad to look back on your life and wonder what it would be like living without the repercussions of a disorder. Since my family cannot enjoy that luxury, we must ask even deeper questions. What it would be like if only I had had a diagnosis sooner? In my support group, I see younger people and I am always happy for them. I am not happy for their disorder, but for their proactive ability to deal with their problems. They aren't in denial, and they have the best chance at overcoming adversity. I think support groups work for so many reasons, but probably the biggest one is just realizing that there are others out there with similar problems. I had been burned, wrecked my motorcycle, and been in a major car accident, and I wasn't even drinking age. Lord only knows what was in for this fool. Thank God I don't like beer. I am getting closer to my Vivid Blue.

Chapter 12. Learning What Forgiveness Is All About

In my search for a Vivid Blue, I have come to the conclusion that I need forgiveness for a great many things. I can honestly say that my very presence here on earth has affected the lives of other people, and dare I say that at a minimum, some people have incurred great pain. None of it was by intent, but I'm sure that isn't even weighed as a factor in the equation. I choose not to go into specifics for many reasons, but the main one is clear to all, that words will just cause more pain.

When looking for forgiveness, words fail in the eyes of the victims. Almost nothing can be said that can justify an action that has caused somebody pain. In the victim's eyes, these actions are reason enough to become hard and unforgiving. It is human nature to bear resentment. I do feel that the person or persons who have been directly affected have the right to feel however they wish. Evidently a person's overwhelming remorse isn't enough to change a bad situation. In my case, it most assuredly isn't enough. Karma is a bitch, and mine bites hard. I have learned positive ways to forgive myself and deal with my own actions. But I don't expect the same of others toward me.

The intent of this chapter is not to absolve anything I have done, but to help you understand it is okay to forgive yourself, even if no one else will. Many people in this world make mistakes that hurt others. It happens every day. That statement isn't meant to belittle a situation, it is meant to put everything into perspective. Even if others cannot move past a certain point, you have to be strong and move past it for yourself. It does no good to dwell in the past, or make today miserable because somebody else wants it that way. Your past actions may have added a whole bunch of people to the list who wish to see you fall or suffer. That should give you more determination to move past your stumbling blocks. Learn from your mistakes and move on. When you forgive yourself and realize there was never any malice or intent behind your mistake, accept it and move on. Sometimes rethinking it is all you can do, and it just proves how strong you really are mentally and sometimes even physically.

This chapter isn't really about me, but about what you can do for your own sake. The only time I will touch this subject, and what I take from this is the knowledge I rest in. That is I never did anything wrong and even if I did, I never meant any harm. I think too many people are judging me in the harshest ways when they weren't there and don't even know what really happened. People are going to read into this just what they want to believe. It is subject to personal interpretation, and that will be staunchly harsh too.

What do I know? I'm just trying to convey to all the people out there that they can get past a major mistake in life. There comes a time when you have to move forward and realize you cannot change the past. The present is here, and it is all we can do to live in the moment. I am writing this as a positive-minded person. I will not allow myself the time or the energy to write about history when I am down or depressed. It is a formula that works for me.

So for me, Vivid Blue is about the act of forgiveness. It is the understanding that we cause others pain and sometimes immeasurable suffering. Vivid Blue highlights what it is like to open our eyes to the fact that we need to be forgiven, and more importantly, we need to forgive others too. Remember, you cannot receive forgiveness if you aren't the type of person to give forgiveness. You cannot have it your way and just say, "Oh, I want you to forgive my infraction," but forgiving your many "little infractions" is different. It might be that all the little infractions add up to much more than the big infraction. Remember that one big mistake with no intent to hurt another might weigh less than thousands of little intentional hurts. In my case, none of this is meant to sound like I don't have a conscience or that I am not sorry. I am. I just don't know what else to do but move forward. The search for a Vivid Blue has taken me deep inside a world of regret and wishful thinking. The concept of Vivid Blue required me to look at my actions and come to the conclusion that my decisions weren't based solely on how they affected me. I had to realize my decisions in life

79

affect everyone.

Chapter 13. Consistency and Dependability

In my youth, I never thought about the quality of a job in correlation to my work. I didn't do a good job just to do the job correctly. I suspect it was my immaturity riding higher than my OCD. Everything was done because I thought I needed to make my boss happy. Owning my own business has made me rethink my actions and my past, including all I have ever done and all that I am doing right now. Writing a chapter on my early work experiences has been a challenging task. In doing so, I have been rewarded with a clearer perspective on my past. At the same time, there are questions that open up like a rip in a sheet. These are the same questions anybody would ask when looking back on their life. I wonder if anybody ever gives credit to the plausible explanation "It just happened" for their haphazard unraveling of life. The thought of being in the present with no explanation for how we got here is just as frightening as not having a plan for the future. It seems my life just evolved. My early work days evolved too. It took seventeen years to get the right medicines, and that's when I realized I would not be in control until I got the medicines I needed. But I am also of the opinion that sometimes the medicines don't exist yet, or the problem is just too dire.

I do not take pride in learning lessons. I feel most of the lessons are things I should have known beforehand. In fact, looking back at all my lessons, I cannot believe I didn't drag my fingers along the ground like a Neanderthal. I can only wonder what I should know now but fail to realize. I am sure of one thing: life will evolve to a point where I will look back and say, "This I should have known."

By now I don't have to convince you that my accidents and my burns had a big influence on my life. As a result of them, I started to act a lot more mature than most people my age—that is, when I wasn't melting down from my depression/schizo disorders. Unfortunately, some if not most of my success was just an act. Yet it was the only good thing going for me. The adults were starting to see me as a kid with promise. The OCD made me work hard at any task I set my mind to. Still, my one and only goal in my work was to make my boss happy. Here is the part that bites the most: the OCD worked against me if I had things other than work on my mind. The mood swings had to be a factor too. I didn't know how to control it, and nobody else did, either. Admittedly, we didn't know there was a problem. We knew we had to control it, and we just made it through the times the best way we knew how. It's called coping. I always say, you cope until you get the diagnosis, and then you can start to manage. It took years to get my diagnosis. So I coped and looked for reasons to be happy. I smoked a lot of dope. Lord, I smoked a lot of dope.

I know now that there are reasons you have to try very hard to look for the positive in every bad situation. I didn't see this little revelation as a goal until late in my life. As a matter of fact, it wasn't until I was writing my book that I fully realized this little tidbit. I also didn't realize the importance of your work ethic. I have been known to be a hard worker when things are going my way, but when things are falling apart, I just give up. Learning that little morsel about myself was priceless. I needed some things to go my way. I made it very far because I was dependable, despite my OCD and mood swings.

When I was young, I had a paper route with the *Huntsville Times*. I felt very fortunate to be a little business tycoon. It instilled values that later proved invaluable in everything I did. The effort it took to write this book is my proof. My brother is the one who got me the job, for it was he who came home to trumpet the news. I was a little jealous of his paper route. Lance's boss said there was another opening, but the route was a little shorter. His manager said, "It would be perfect for Lance's little brother." It might have been shorter, but it was difficult to work due to the many hills. Nonetheless, I was very pleased to have the job, and I kept it for several years.

Other early jobs I had were delivering auto parts and working at McDonald's. At every job, I learned the simple but time-proven method of rising to the top: hard work. Yep, the same thing most people do every day. My whole family followed this pattern. My father worked two jobs, and my grandmother started out as an English teacher and worked her way up to head librarian for the Mira Mesa branch library in San Diego.

Listing some mini occupations here wouldn't do anything but show my dysfunctions in a pathetic light. It goes without saying that a person with a few disorders probably has a few problems getting along in a work environment. I learned the usual lessons that are necessary to hold a position with responsibility. I would like to state that there were many things I could be proud of too. In my search I learned that life is all about perspective. My father always told me that if you look for the bad in a person, you will find it. I think that is true. Still, if I were to say anything, I would sum it all up with a note about my lack of consistency. I could have been better at a lot of things. However, I always completed the task, if at all possible. One thing was still lacking in it all: I needed approval from high up. It went along with how I felt about the burns. If I could only get past the feeling that I had done something stupid, and, even more important, stop thinking about it cyclically, I would have been much better off.

Having all my disorders, especially my OCD, and not knowing it might have been a blessing at times. There was a side that made me continue moving about until the job was done. One place it helped was working at a video store. I was able to keep that job longer, and maybe the reason was that I was promoted to manager. Well, I might not have technically made it to manager, but I was the only full-time employee for years, so in my mind, I was it. In any case, at the risk of repeating myself, I did have a multitude of problems that weren't obvious to everybody but that still caused havoc on my life. I also kept my job by being honest and dependable.

The video store was a flat-roofed, tan-bricked building that was almost exactly what you would picture in a small town. The large posters lining the windows encouraged everybody to come inside. We rented both VCR tapes and machines. We kept a large assortment of new releases. We never got into the sale of candy or junk food, and it was probably better that way. The store was on the edge of the historic section of our city in a very populated area. Our store was aptly if unimaginatively named Five Points Video. I'm having a hard time describing the place because its main feature was its lack of uniqueness. It was very comfortable in its delivery, and that was why it was so successful. It had everything to do with the owners' philosophy of treating people right.

In the evenings, my boss, Murray, would let us stay and watch videos after store hours. We, of course, had to abide by his rules. We had a great time watching all those old movies. To my recollection, all we did was smoke a little pot, but at a reunion in my forties, I found out that I'd been left out of many illegal activities. A few of my friends were doing things I had no idea about. Thank God I didn't know. With my OCD, there's no telling how addicted I would have become. I got into those activities later in life anyway, but it was better that I didn't start at such a young age. Anyway, if we cleaned up the store and rewound the VCR tapes, we were allowed to watch a couple of movies. It was always past nine thirty when the movies got started, and they were usually new releases. I never took ones that the customers wanted, but if somebody returned one just before closing, it might not get on the shelf until the morning. We were lucky that way.

During the mornings it was my job to restock the shelves. Most of the tapes were from customers who had dropped off the previous night's rentals in the drop box. Almost every weekday morning, my boss and I had a blast playing along with *The Price Is Right*. We would tally up the prices of the Showcase Showdown, and whoever was closest wouldn't have to buy lunch. We always got very close, and we almost always traded off on lunch. Of course, if my boss won, we got a simple lunch, and if I won, we got a pizza because I hated to have to move my car and lose my morning parking spot.

I like to think I was Murray's best employee, and I fancied myself manager even if it wasn't official. Who cares? Life was good until the competition came in and the big chain stores came in to town. We eventually had to close, but it was a great business for three or four years of my life. I learned a lot. Murray taught me more about business than anybody, and he is probably the reason I am so successful today. Still, I went in and out of my phases, and nobody

84

but my closest relatives knew I had a serious problem. If my job stayed steady and my money stayed steady, I seemed to be fine. It was when there were external factors, like when my dog died or other triggers, that I had problems. During these problems things got really out of hand, and Murray knew it. I think he was wise beyond his years, but he could still see the good in people. I like to think good people exist and are more plentiful than the bad ones. In today's world it makes you wonder.

One morning after I had become manager, I opened the store and started to tally the drawer and restock the tapes. After about an hour, I went to tally up the deposit from the night before so Murray could take it to the bank later that day. That was when I ran into a serious problem. All the money was gone! I called the girl who'd closed the night before, and she told me she'd left the money in the drawer. I called Murray, and he said that he hadn't come in early to collect the money. There wasn't any other way to look at it: we must have had a thief in our midst. What was worse, it kept happening for a period of months. We changed the locks, but the crook kept coming back. We tried to hide the money, but somehow the crook found it. We were losing a lot of money, Murray was getting very upset, and there was nothing we could do to figure it out. Murray or I would call the police, who came and did their usual thing. The detective and Murray talked. When they could not figure out how the crook did it, they figured with increased security and an alarm system, the crook would not return.

As time passed, the crook took action. This time he got larger amounts of cash. It would seem that he knew which days to hit the cash drawer to get his hands on the store's money. The police and Murray were stumped as to how the thief was entering the store. It seemed to be an inside job. This went on for at least a couple more months, when finally the police wanted everybody who worked for Murray to take a lie detector test. I did and was told I failed. I don't think I really failed; I think they told me that because I ran scared like everything was my fault or I was stupid for blowing myself up. Anyway, I was told I failed.

This couldn't be. I wasn't taking the money. Murray said that he knew I was not responsible and that he wouldn't press charges if it were me. Well, I was smart enough to know that just because Murray didn't press charges didn't mean the police couldn't go ahead and press charges anyway. I know the police were sure I was taking the money. I know that my record of being a good person was a little tarnished by my drug usage. I was scared, and I didn't want to hurt Murray. He was good to me and I respected him. This is another time in my life that I look back on and see the paranoia going full blast. It is probably the very reason the police suspected me. It all goes back to the times in high school when the parking guard always thought I was doing something wrong. You act like you're doing something wrong and you will be accused of it. One night Murray asked me to bring the money to him after closing the store, and I did. The police pulled me over with the money. Murray had to explain to the police that he did indeed ask me to take the money to him after closing the store. What a mess! Would anybody believe this SABP mixed-up PTSD kid? They let me go because I didn't do it.

One day, after quaking in my boots, Murray called me and said that the police had caught the guy. I think it was the boyfriend of the girl who worked at the store, and the police were questioning both of them downtown. The boyfriend would have gotten away with it if he hadn't come back for more money.

Only one thing saved me from this bad situation: how long I had worked at the video store. If my track record had been less than outstanding, Murray could have laid me off just to eliminate the possibility that I was the thief. I would never have had been able to build such a great reputation if it weren't for the consistency of my work. My OCD was seemingly a benefit, but only in retrospect. That is in the big picture. When I think about all the little things, like worrying about my car making a noise or where it was parked, I think my life would have been so much better if I could have just relaxed. I drove myself nuts with all the little details that didn't add up to a hill of beans. But like I said, my OCD (in the big picture) drove me to be consistent.

At that time, all factors in my life were a constant, and I was moderately happy. Unfortunately for me, it would take another two decades to figure out that I had PTSD and schizoaffective disorder. I still think we should have known about the OCD, but we weren't paying attention. I wonder if I would have been able to go farther in my career had I known. I am sure the transition to my next job would have been easier. Thankfully, I have always had my father and my grandmother as two positive role models in my life. I can only think that my honesty played a key part in my search for a Vivid Blue. Just because you have a few sizeable disorders doesn't mean you have to compromise your dignity. I heard a saying once and I will always think it is true: they can't take away your dignity; it is something you give away.

Chapter 14. Starting a Business

I think I can, I think I can. Really? What made me think I could run a business at such a young age? I sure did have an attitude on top of pretending that life was perfect. Oh, I did pretend too! I was only fooling myself. In contrast, I work very hard at keeping everything in line today, and I hope it shows. That said, mental illness brings lots of problems to the table when it comes to starting a business. Undiagnosed issues are always the worst. In the case of my first business, though, I really don't think I had it that bad. Actually, my undiagnosed OCD was seemingly beneficial. I will not go so far as to say it made up for my other idiosyncrasies. I could pretend to be in control of my schizoaffective disorders, but I could not do it for days on end. I learned to cope because nobody knew of my situation, and my real diagnosis was yet unknown. I don't think my business suffered from the whirlwind of problems. That was a miracle. Most people with OCD don't get miracles until they find the right meds, like the ones that got me to stop chewing my fingernails. I have always kidded myself in thinking the best way to handle a mental illness is to pretend like you don't have one. This sentiment was developed from analyzing the days I operated really well. More times than not, I have said you just cope until you are diagnosed. It is then that you manage. Well, in order to truly manage, you have to accept that life is just that way. Without fully believing you can do something about your situation, you're better off coping. At least that way, you are not feeling sorry for yourself. Believe me, I have felt and sometimes still feel sorry for myself, so much so it is immobilizing.

After my video store days, I was approached by a retired colonel to start a tool and equipment rental store. I was a little too sure of myself, and I really cannot understand why. I understand why he hired me. I just don't understand why I was so sure of myself. My all-around success rate at this time was high, but this business venture would make it plummet. It was the first time that I was really aware of my drug problem. I still thought I could handle the drugs, but now I realized I had to work to hide it and work to pay for it. I could no longer play the sneak-away-at-work-and-get-high routine. The days required full-time attention, and that left only nights (and some days that didn't require social interaction) for my drug pursuits and self-medication. By nighttime I was exhausted. However, I think it was a good time to be OCD without knowing it. It really paid off by my impressing the colonel, and it really paid off in setting up the business. In retrospect, most of the time that I thought I was being super productive, I was really spinning my wheels. I had so much to do, and thankfully I had the energy to do it. Thanks to my OCD, I worked tirelessly at it. South Parkway Rentals was a go.

Before there were any customers, setting up the business was more fun than work. It was professional by every stretch of the imagination. I loved the responsibility and the satisfaction of doing an honest day's work. I had to work more uncounted ten-hour days for that business than for any other job, and it was worth it. Because I was a salaried employee, I never kept track of the hours. I did, however, think of the business as mine, and that was part of my downfall. I was only the manager (well, there was some financial investment loaned to me by my father), and I should not have acted like I was an outright owner. In retrospect, I think my OCD and bipolar behaviors were starting to show their ugly heads. Their control of me got in the way of business. I am surprised the owners didn't see the signs. Maybe they did.

Anyway, I hope by now you're back to wondering more about the rental business. It was really a franchise operation, and we were suckered a little. The owners were following the advice of a guy from Dayton, Ohio. I was the one doing all the work and keeping everybody happy. It is hell making a colonel happy when you aren't in the army and don't have a bunch of little privates running around. He never gave me a break. I could never do anything right. I was never offered any help except from Todd, who helped with mechanical equipment repair.

I was a very cocky young man, and at the time I really butted heads with the owners. The colonel spoke for all the owners, but I knew one of the owners would always voice his opinion privately to the colonel. He never had the courage to say his piece in my presence. I don't know if he thought he would be undermining the colonel's authority or if he was intimidated by me. Either way, it bothered me. I knew the record keeping, checking, and payroll were going to be a problem from the beginning. I was having the hardest time getting money for the equipment already, and I couldn't risk having financial problems right from the get-go. It wasn't that I am lousy at record keeping. I just needed a formal system that produced a carbon copy of every check written so I could justify every expense. I also needed it for tax purposes, and I could smell little things like depreciation of equipment coming down the pike.

I made an executive decision to buy a complete accounting system without the owners' permission. It was a very expensive system, but it was all-inclusive. It did all the things I mentioned, all the way down to taxes and even depreciation of equipment. I thought I could hide the expense in the cost of the equipment and make the owners happy by reporting everything in logical format. Well, I didn't think it out too far because the system reported itself, and the new checks gave it away too. They figured out how much I'd paid for it and blew a gasket. It was the start of a long line of their many disappointments. Eventually they told me they wanted to hire a new manager to replace me. They said they would make me assistant manager. I balked at this decision and resented being demoted.

I had a very hard time swallowing the loss of my managerial status. I'd started the business from nothing and taken it all the way to having customers and renting out the equipment. It really wasn't fair. They never offered to have somebody help me do the job. It was always doing this, doing that, but it was never "we will get somebody to help you." Like I said, they did hire my good friend Todd, who was great in small engine repair. Still, they never got me managerial help and they certainly had money for that. So I quit. I remember sitting on my father's deck and telling him why the business was going to fail. I wasn't so cocky as to believe that it would have succeeded with me, I just believed at that moment the owners were better at making bad decisions. As it turned out, the manager they replaced me with was an embezzler. The checking system I installed caught him.

During this point in my life, I would have been in denial if any doctor had voiced suspicion of any of my disorders. My life was out of hand, and I was like a bull in a china shop. The ancient Greek aphorism "Know thyself" is a priceless motto. There are many good doctors with excellent training in spotting mental illness, and all you have to do is be open and willing to keep working with them until you get the right medications. For me, it did take some time to find the right medications, but I think it will happen for most people who need medicine and stay the course in finding it. Hopefully it will be done in time to get you where you want to be.

I was lucky. I would never have gone to college if it had not been for losing the rental business. I gave a little to gain a whole lot. I was very hopeful at this time in my life, and it paid off. Hope is such a wonderfully optimistic trait to possess, and I can't say enough about it. I always hope tomorrow is better than today. I was definitely going in the right direction toward finding my Vivid Blue.

Chapter 15. My First Place

Maya Angelou said, "The ache for home lives in all of us, the safe place where we can go as we are and not be questioned." I found my place, as short-lived as it might have been. I thundered in with the recklessness of a brash young adult. I had nothing in savings and little prospect of a future. The time spent outside my apartment was greater than the time spent inside. I had no clue what my future was going to hold.

When I got the job as manager of the tool and equipment rental store, I got a salary that was compensatory for the position. Pennies from heaven and pounds from hell; I thought I was rich. At the time, I had never seen a paycheck that large. My dad, a supposedly silent partner, warned them not to give me that grand salary. He wanted me to build to it. But the colonel and leader of the pack thought it would give me incentive. It was one decision the brass nailed right on the head. I wanted to earn as many hours as possible. Well, not exactly true because I was salaried, but I did want the business to be successful. I figured with that success would come more money and prestige. Soon I found a hole burning in my pocket. I couldn't wait to move out of my parents' house. I needed to learn all my lessons the hard way. What's the saying? There are 1 percent who knew better, 10 percent who learned by watching others, and 89 percent who learned the hard way. Well, in this case I was among the 89 percent.

One of the telltale signs of my OCD was the disorganized manner in which I made the transition. It was a haphazard move with no planning. I was obsessed with getting into the apartment, and I never got a full truckload of furniture when I had the chance. I made many trips. It seems ridiculous to have made as many trips as I did for only one room of furniture. I just picked up a small amount of stuff and off I went. Of course, there was nobody to help me. I couldn't ask my brother, as he was in the navy. Dad was working all the time, and the only help he was going to give me was cosigning on the lease. I had very few friends because I was still a loner. I remember moving everything from my second-floor bedroom down to the truck myself. I needed Mom's help moving some of it up to the second-floor apartment. She had an awful time helping me move my mattress. The most important things like my stereo, television, and dresser made it the first night. The rest came over in several more trips over the next few days.

It was a really nice apartment in a nice section of town. I really don't think my paranoia was showing its ugly head, because I used to leave the windows open. I didn't have to worry about any neighbors. Actually, they probably were worried about some young punk moving in and thinking he owned the place. I never thought about anybody except the two lesbians who lived across the street from me. We waved, but that soon stopped due to a really strange incident. It manifested into a growing sense of avoiding them, but that might have been normal too. The next-door neighbor complained about my stereo, but I promised to keep it down. The biggest issue was I had a major problem with dope. I smoked it at every opportunity, even during lunch. I would rush home, fix a sandwich, and take a toke or two. I would get high as a kite and go back to work. I would do something out of the limelight for hours. I did this until we had actual customers. Then I was afraid they would be able to detect my buzz. I thought I was super productive with my buzz. I rationalized that I "got into my work." I didn't know I had OCD or mood swings, so it really never got too bad to handle.

I managed to party every night and twice on the weekend. Having a place to party is a young person's dream. At least it was my dream until it crashed down around me. I had nowhere to go but down, and it was very evident. It was just a matter of how far down I was going to go. For a while I didn't have to worry about being "the boy who blew himself up." I think I overcompensated, and I became a little monster. The few friends I had were very successful in my eyes, and now I was too. I played the trump card of being manager. I never thought it could be taken away from me, and I never thought about what I would do if it happened. I never thought about the embarrassment that losing the job would bring.

What can I say? It happened. Actually, I should say I quit. They wanted to make me assistant manager. I wasn't going to be assistant manager of the business I helped set up. I thought I would get another job as manager in another establishment. I thought somebody would hire me at the same pay to do the same thing. I never thought I would need the pay from the assistant manager position to pay my bills. I only thought of my pride. I wasn't really thinking at all, I was reacting. I was probably close to melting down from my disorders too. I know the drugs were hurting the situation, but I was using them as a means of escape. I had payments, a drug problem, undiagnosed mental disorders, and now no job.

I was out to prove the owners had made a mistake in their decision. I didn't own up to my decision to quit. I shifted all the blame on them for demoting me. As long as I felt it was their problem, I was going to flounder. That is beside the point. I answered several want ads for highly motivated managers. I thought I was the perfect candidate. I was young, seemingly smart, and eager. What else could they want? My references were good. At least, references from my recent past were good. Of course, I couldn't include the rental store venture because I'd quit, though I felt sure the colonel would give me a good reference anyway, especially since they were going to make me assistant manager. So what else could these new employers want? I didn't think about a track record. Mine was a complete flop. I had to admit it flopped in record time too. They asked me why I was looking for a management position and asked me to list my qualifications. I bombed interview after interview. I became depressed.

It got to the point where I was running out of money, so I had to make critical choices. For me, a critical choice was how to get drugs. I smoked dope to deal with bad situations. I'd done this since I'd blown myself up. I remember choosing to buy a huge bag of dope with the last of my money. I thought even if they turned off the lights, I could still get high. Wow, my stupidity astounds me. Oops, there I go again. I shouldn't call myself stupid. This one time, though, I think I am justified. What was I going to do? I didn't have a clue. I wasn't even trying to look for a job anymore. I was depressed, by every clinical definition.

My mother was worried about me and bringing food to my front door. She kept saying Dad wanted to talk to me. That was laughable. How on earth did he think I was going to talk to him? The last time I saw him, I was blubbering on his deck about losing my job. I wasn't about to run by and chat. I barely answered the door for free groceries. I was starting to sleep for most of the day and never answered the phone. I didn't want to talk to the few friends I had. It was their turn to say, "We still have our jobs, and you aren't *manager*."

I finally started getting collection calls. I owed money. It doesn't take long to run out of money and accumulate debt. I can't believe I took out a cash advance to pay the rent payment. That is the grim reaper of finances. I only did this a couple of times before I hit my limit. I was facing bankruptcy. In retrospect, I probably was facing jail time too. I don't think you are supposed to do what I did.

Finally my landlord said I was being evicted. He told me he had no choice and I had until the end of the month to vacate. Dad had cosigned for the apartment, but he wasn't going to pay a nickel until my finances were under control. "Under control" meant he was no longer responsible for my debts. I had just a few days to figure out what I was going to do. Life in the banyan swamp was treacherous, and the alligators were hungry.

Mom came by again and told me I had one more chance with Dad. It was a double message—she was tired of telling me and he wanted to see me, *now*. I knew she was serious by the way she told me. There are times my when my mother can be serious and I know not to mess around. This was one. It is kind of like an incident when I was about twelve and I put Mom in a wrestling hold. She said she had to make dinner and couldn't fool around. I told her she'd better do something. She flipped me on the vacuum cleaner.

I still didn't go home. I was my own man, and I was going to find out everything the hard way. I promptly set out to get wasted. That's when I heard a knock at my door. I don't know what possessed me to answer it with such a buzz, but I did. I can only imagine what my father was thinking when he told me he didn't want to see me trashed. He was very disappointed and he wanted me to sober up. He also wanted to talk to me. I knew that.

I remember thinking my father would never picture me as having any fortitude. The most I could hope for would be Brando screaming for Stella. In reality, I would have to settle for a drunk staggering through the streets. I was "the boy who blew himself up," and now I was just a loser. It wasn't the worst thing that has happened to me by far, but I was really depressed. I was even a touch suicidal. I thought the world would be better off without me. I had been thinking that way for a long time. I just didn't verbalize it.

I sat in my car for what seemed like an hour before going inside to talk to my father. I rehearsed what I was going to say. It didn't matter, I didn't want to move back home. But deep down, I knew I had no options. I wanted to control everything. I had no poker chips left, and Dad knew it. Finally we were face to face. Oh, what a long time coming. I felt two feet tall. Dad kept his cool. It was unusual for him. He used to scream at my brother. As a matter of fact, that was why Lance had gone into the navy. Long story short, I don't remember all the details of our conversation, but I ended up telling him that I did try to find a job, but nobody would give me one. He listened and grumbled some things. He really wasn't hard on me. I was harder on myself about the job. His biggest problem was catching me wasted. He'd suspected it, but now that his suspicions were confirmed, he didn't know what to do about it.

He finally said he was going to make me an offer. He would pay my debts if I moved back home and went to college. Not junior college, but the University of Alabama in Huntsville. The deal was home and school. No in-betweens. And there was one more catch. If I didn't graduate, I owed him every penny he spent.

I actually said no. I said, "I can make it without college." He said the offer would only be made once. I hemmed and hawed and pondered for an eternity, and then I said I would go to school. Then I added, "But I'm not moving back home." He said, "No deal." I think I might have been able to keep my independence if I hadn't been sloshed when he came to my door. He said twice that that was a deal breaker. I thought for a long moment. I knew I owed everybody and their brother money. So I took the deal. Dad cringed when he found out I had a credit card and had taken out cash advances to pay my rent.

I started classes as soon as I could. I didn't want to test my father after he'd paid my bills. I was grateful, and I knew school was my best option for getting decent employment. I have no clue how I got past my phenomenal failures. I did remember my debts, and I was quite sure it was easier to go to class than to pay back a fortune. In my first class, I was caught daydreaming, and the professor told me he was going to fail me. I also got a thirty-three on an exam. I barely made a C. I knew I was in for some work.

The older I get, the easier it is to see what a gift it was to have the opportunity to go to an advanced university. My father knew I had troubles, but he also knew I had no other choice but survive. For a long moment, I was blind to all the possibilities, both negative and positive. In my search, I learned that the answers aren't always visible. The Vivid Blue is the knowledge that I trusted family to help me out of a very bad situation. Vivid Blue is also an acknowledgement that I have family willing to help. I was old enough for my father to have walked away from me. He could have let me learn my lessons the hard way. He chose to offer me a better path. That was the first time in a long time that I made a good decision. I had to get my degree, even though I didn't know how I was going to do it. What made it worse, I didn't know what I was going to do with it. I never knew I had disorders to overcome; I never knew I was coping and not managing. I graduated when I was twenty-eight, and I learned what bipolar disorder was when they diagnosed me somewhere around age thirty-two. Wow, how things changed in just a few short years. My Vivid Blue surely would have been better had I known my problems a decade sooner.

Chapter 16. Never Forget

The power of words is immeasurable. They are the magical keys that allow us to live in the past, the present, and the future. They can make us happy or they can make us sad. They have the power to mold us, mend us, and even break us. Words are the necessary tools to shape us as individuals. Sometimes words are not inspirational. Sometimes words hurt. The pain that words bring can last a lifetime. Hurtful words can come in any form, but I am really referring to a derogatory remark or even a sideways compliment that lets the taker assume what they will. Whatever is muttered is subjected to the simple little law: "You never have to apologize for something you don't say." All too often I am reminded of this, and I ever so humbly slink away, hoping to be forgiven. Maybe I will be lucky, and people will be distracted and forget. Maybe, just maybe, I can turn around all that pain from my ill used words and say something right.

Trying to say the right thing to a schizoaffective person is like gambling. You never know how he or she is going to take it. It is that way for me, at least; maybe I am just superimposing my problems on a group of people. Then again, maybe trying to say the right thing to any mentally ill person would fit into that category. I do, however, think it takes training and plenty of thought to say the right things at the right time. Then again, the reverse may be true. SABP people have a harder time saying the right thing.

I had my opportunity to say something right at the same time that I heard the most devastating words. I never knew these words were inspirational until many years later, when I turned them around and made them work for me. I use this as a reference when I am in the hospital for anything. It really works for schizoaffective problems, and all the way through my kidney stone removal. I hope that my words on paper will do justice to the story and maybe save somebody many years of frustration and grief. It is also my hope that something I say will in turn help that person's loved ones deal with hardships. It is my belief that everybody deserves a better life, and learning through others is the key to that life. The people who have inspired me are at the heart of this abstract idea.

In my times in the hospital, I realized you need to hold your head up high. There are many things a schizoaffective person could feel embarrassed about. A person suffering from paranoia (at least my kind) feels spotlighted. I don't want to be watched. I want to be left alone, and solitude never comes. I will set the stage even better by saying my schizoaffective behavior wasn't suspect or even an issue in my mood swings. We thought my depression was due to my losing a business. My OCD was only attached to my habit of chewing my fingernails, and to some cyclical thoughts that kept me wrapped up in berating everything I set forth to do (except the smallest of jobs). I had no better alternative than to just cope. I know that sounds a little trite, but heck, it was going on ten or so years, and the main residual effect was the "I must be stupid" part, not the fear of explosions. So my PTSD had probably become more tolerable.

In my younger days, the most notable person I had the privilege of knowing was a lady named Helen. When I first met her, I thought she was a frail, timid person. I knew she had to be in her late sixties. Her age made an impression on me, not because I cared, but because she was so much older than my mother. I heard my mother mention her name many times before I met her, and I expected her to be in her forties. Above all, Helen was a very nice, pleasant woman with a lot of character. Nothing I say should detract from her intelligence or her being, because she had wisdom beyond her years.

Some days stand out in your memory, and the day I met Helen is one of them. I was in the process of running my tool and equipment rental store when she and my mother stopped by to say hello. Truth be known, Mom had brought her by to do a little bragging. All mothers brag, and mine is no exception. I'm lucky that way. I see the love in my mother's eyes when she talks about me. At times I wish I didn't have to live up to her expectations. But without them, I would be a failure. Be that as it may, with this business venture, I didn't rise to the occasion. I couldn't stop the wheels of time from turning, and I watched my business crumble before my eyes. Just a few short months after the rental store opened, I was out looking for other ways to earn a living.

Without a formal education, I wasn't going to get very far, and I knew it. I moped around my apartment until they almost evicted me. Actually, I was in the process of being evicted when my father made me the offer of my life. He said he would pay all my bills if I would promise to get my college degree. I agreed, but you know all that. Going back to school left me with a serious need for money, so I went back to mowing lawns for income. Helen was one of my best customers. She had a very large yard, and it was quite a chore to mow properly. It had to be done right. Her husband was a colonel, and he wanted it a certain way. To say he was particular about the details is an understatement.

One day I was informed that Helen had cancer. I was taken completely off guard. I must admit that I was a little naïve, and at the time, and I didn't think anybody survived the disease. I assumed the same would hold true for Mom's dear friend, and once again I had reason to fear the big C. Mom told me that Helen wanted me to take her to the hospital for treatment. They had been discussing this for some time, and they wanted to know if I was okay with that idea. Mom was to run the idea past me first. When it was time for an answer, I agreed. Being young almost implied, by some law of nature, that I wouldn't know what this job entailed. The first thing I did was call up Helen and say yes.

Cancer isn't the sort of thing a young guy thinks about, and he thinks about it even less when he's in the middle of school. Sure, it did float in and out of my mind, but usually it was about the time I drove Helen to the hospital. Nothing could stop it from being a predominate force weighing heavily on Helen's mind. In the beginning, the trips were nothing more than routine. Of course, I always told her I didn't want any compensation. But she always said, "That is what we agreed upon," and she always paid me the fee. As I get older, I have to remind myself she wanted it that way. I have always wondered why she wanted me to take her. It was a strange arrangement.

The months passed, and I could tell the chemotherapy was taking a toll on her body. She was having radiation treatment in tandem, so as a result, she started to lose her hair. There was no doubt Helen was in for more than just a fight. It would be her last good fight. She wasn't winning. I kept telling her it would be fine. What did I know? I was young, and at the time I thought I was invincible. I wouldn't have known disaster if it had stared me in the face. It was the time in my life when I was the most naive. Helen never let on how scared she was, but I know she had to be scared.

The treatments could not be avoided, and to say they were obligatory is as redundant as the trips were becoming. All were in the morning, and we usually had lunch afterward. One day we arrived early for her treatments, and we were greeted with a long line of people. That wasn't the norm. Usually the hospital didn't make their patients wait. They had an excellent track record, and we knew something was amiss. We ended up waiting a couple of hours, and we still weren't any closer to being called back. By this time I could tell Helen was getting upset. She was starting to fidget, so I wheeled her around the corner to see what was wrong. There was only one orderly, and he looked quite busy. He assured us it wouldn't be much longer.

Nevertheless, Helen couldn't wait any longer. She had tried to make it to the restroom on her own and had accidentally soiled herself. She asked me to be stern and get her help. I did what I could, but there was nobody to assist. We waited for what seemed like an eternity, and I got exceedingly impatient. Finally I demanded that they do something, and I explained how urgently she needed help. The orderly threw me some towels and other supplies from the laundry closet and said in haste, "Get what you need." I went back to Helen and told her that we were going to be okay.

What happened next was beyond one of life's little lessons. You see, I was a twenty-five-year-old male who had never had more than a stomachache his whole life (except for my burns and ruptured Appendix). It was apparent that Helen's bodily functions weren't working, and her treatment was making her quite sick. My job had just become more complicated: I was a personal nurse. I had to help her in ways I wasn't prepared. As we cleaned her up, she said to me, "I don't work anymore." Those were the life-changing words that shattered my psyche. It was such a simple little phrase, but the most devastating of all. She said it so softly, yet it couldn't have been any louder. I was speechless. I knew I had to say something. I stuttered and I stammered. I almost choked, and then I coughed. I looked up, and there was no sign of the Helen I once knew. Her visage was pale and completely lacking in color. Her eyes were sad. Somehow I managed to utter something correct. All I said was, "We are going to pretend this never happened." And we did. It seemed we had no choice.

Pretending is something you do as a child, not as an adult. Adults have to be courageous and divert their minds to something more pleasant. I wasn't capable of that at such a young age. I have OCD, and all I heard was, "I don't work anymore." I mulled it over. Now I know what I am supposed to do in situations like that, but I didn't back then. As I get older, it gets easier to tell myself to think better thoughts. I was never taught this technique. I learned it on my own. Besides, it takes years of practice. Now the phrase reemerges and I have to squelch it. I hear it: "I don't work anymore." How was I ever going to get past that one simple phrase? What a mess I found myself in, and I sure did want to forget it. Luxuries don't come easy as an adult.

I get past those words by remembering when I met Helen. I don't consider it pretending. I consider it granting a wish. A person always wishes to be remembered in a favorable light. That first day, I was wrong about her. I think how easy it was for me to assume she was so much older than my mother. Ultimately I came to the conclusion that you shouldn't judge a person by their age. What a mistake it is to remember somebody by their last few days. Oh, the lessons one person can teach! Helen helped me through the first few years of college, and then she went on and opened my eyes well into my adult years. The kind and caring person is now a memory. It is a good memory and one that I visit often. I will always remember her standing next to a post and smiling.

My disorders make me feel like screaming. I want to do just the opposite of what Helen did that day. I want to scream, "I don't work," and I want (maybe even expect) people to understand. I know it falls on deaf ears at times. My own brother will always comment and say little things like "It's all about you" and bring me back to reality. Yes, my paranoia does manifest itself in a sort of selfish way.

I do need to put it into check, and usually it requires external forces to get me started. I do my levelheaded best not to involve my brother and his wife, because they seem to understand my issues the least. I get a resounding "Get over it" every time. Still, I want to say my body doesn't work like theirs does, and I don't get the opportunity to live without the effects of my disorders driving me in circles.

I never told my mother this story until after Helen had passed away. Helen would have wanted it that way. Mom can understand why. Maybe I shouldn't be putting this in my book, but I really think Helen would understand. It was a monumental lesson for me, and maybe one day I will understand what life is about. It seems to be happening sooner than I expect because I realize the body shuts down a little at a time if you have certain ailments. For example, I am low on my vitamin B and D levels, and certain other medications are throwing my other levels into a spin. Mostly I feel like I am no longer working like I should—never to the point where I raise a white flag, but definitely to the point where I tell the doctor we must do something. I wonder when the time will come that I need help. I know that someday I will be taken care of by somebody who has never seen more than a stomachache. One day I will say with a quiet and humble little voice, "I don't work anymore." That same day, I will look back and remember Helen. When I do, I hope I can go through the embarrassment with as much grace as she did.

I have another story about dealing with my schizoaffective disorder and remembering the people in your life. These stories come so effortlessly that I won't bother you with but just one more. This is a monumental one. It has to do with treating people with respect. I try to give praise whenever I can because it shows respect for a job well done. Going beyond what can be considered good enough is what defines a person's character. I like to think I fall into that category. As a person with schizoaffective disorder and OCD, I can say if going beyond what's necessary is your intent, it is easier. For example, I have some customers who have been with me for many years. Their names are Ken and Georgia. As, a matter of fact, we have a relationship that goes beyond employee and employer. We should—we built it together.

I never knew the first day that Georgia would be the most

instrumental person in my computer business. Over the years she kept telling me to keep with it, and that I was so good at what I did. After a period of time, she even wrote me a letter of commendation, which confirmed how she really felt. There were times I doubted her, and I am sure at times she knew this. She never once had less than the highest expectations of me. She knew what I was capable of if I put my mind to it. Over the years I ended up telling her of my PTSD, OCD, and SABP. She didn't care as long as it didn't interfere with my business. She encouraged me by telling me that these disorders wouldn't stand in my way if I learned how to manage them. Once again, management is a byproduct of a diagnosis and the proper regimen of medication.

Our meeting was never by chance. It was not a simple response to an ad that I placed saying I did computer repair. As luck would have it, I was referred by an elderly gentleman Ken and Georgia happened to trust. It says a lot right from the beginning when you are referred by another customer. As a matter of fact, most of my customers are referrals. I prefer it that way. It is the same in reverse. I know they are good customers if they are referred. Anyway, Georgia called me up, and we made an appointment.

What she asked for was no surprise to me. She had gotten the worst operating system Microsoft ever made, and she had been on the phone for hours with them trying to fix what should have been a simple problem. She isn't the type of person who deals well with this kind of hassle, but she keeps her composure better than most. She stands firm in her beliefs, and she knew she was caught in the middle of a sticky situation. She had just bought the machine from a leading computer company, and she was dealing with them too. Dealing with two companies was a real mess. What she wanted was to change the whole operating system back to an older but vastly more stable system. At the time it was really her best and seemingly only option if she was going to keep the new computer. She was under warranty, so she should have been able to do what she wanted. After all, she wanted to go backward in technology for a very good reason.

I did the work, and on top of that I made sure that she was happy with the hardware she had purchased. The problem was really in the operating system (in my opinion, Vista stinks), and Microsoft would probably even admit that their software didn't work out the way they had hoped. Since then, Georgia has been with me as a customer for many years. She is onto a much newer system, and I still do phone support whenever she has a problem. As a matter of fact, my father and I built her new computer, and I installed the operating system and programs.

There are days I wake and feel that my diagnoses have me cornered. I feel like living up to my prison sentence and being the PTSD, OCD, and schizoaffective person. Invariably I will think I am no good at what I do. And then I think of the letter Georgia wrote me. I start to think I am putting myself down needlessly. Her words of encouragement keep me fueled for my business, and whenever I think I can't do it, I remember there is at least one person who believes I can. I have to remain positive whenever I can to combat my disorders. I realize I am my own worst critic, and over the years I have trained myself to be a negative person. It stems from the burns. Sure, when somebody calls, I put those feelings aside and do the job. It's when I am alone that I do the most damage. Georgia, through the sweetest little compliments, has shown me that she has faith in my ability. Even more, she validates me as a person. My disorders don't in any way make me a bad person, and I don't know why I constantly have to be reminded of that.

People in our lives are our greatest strength. We need to cultivate the good ones and weed out the bad ones. I think about Georgia and Ken all the time, and of all the little things they said that moved me forward. My grandmother did the same thing. I wonder if she saw any of the disorders shining through my youthful exterior. I know she read all the time. Could she have read up on the subject? Heck, being an English teacher and a librarian practically made her a book nerd. I know she kept me positive through college. I think I will try to use the memory of my special people in my search for a Vivid Blue. I still wonder what the "prettiest blue" was that my grandma saw that day when she grabbed my hand, but I can't imagine it being any prettier than the people in our lives. Yet my search continued. I still had a lot to learn.

Chapter 17. I Had Too Much to Lose

Oscillating back and forth on every decision is what I do best. It might be the defining characteristic of a schizoaffective person, but as a patient, I can only speculate. I will say it was easy for my doctors to diagnose the bipolar part of my schizoaffective disorder. At first it was very difficult for them to spot the paranoid behavior because I hid it from everybody but my immediate family. That is the one thing my brother is truly aware of, and he firmly believes that I need to work to control. Also, early on, my immediate family saw my paranoia grow, but they didn't know there was a clinical term for it. They weren't trained to spot a disorder, either. I went into the hospital, and the doctors immediately had the diagnosis. After that, they could help. Of course, it didn't start out that way. It took several months of convincing me to trust them. The real problem was it took even longer for the medicine to work. When it did, I noticed times of brief relief, and I sought out these times for my sanity. Eventually the sane times began to get longer, and the paranoia became shorter. I still have paranoia, but it appears to be better managed. Once again, "managed" can only come after diagnosis.

On the other hand, my father never oscillates. He makes his decisions quickly, without looking back. He is a man of character. He stands tall and strong. His principles never seem to waiver. I know he expects the same from me, but he doesn't always get what he wants. I work very hard at living up to his expectations. While his expectations aren't a secret, he lays down the law silently as though we are supposed to know instinctually what he expects. They are the same principles any upstanding parent has for his children. He learned them from his father when he was a child, and he is trying to pass them on to me. I see it in his brothers, and in my cousins.

My father doesn't talk about his childhood, except in reference to mine. The few times he mentions his childhood, it is only to point out my good fortune. He loves to talk about how things were done by hand or the old-fashioned way. It seems odd, the quantity of words he will use without discussing his past. He had it rough. By the time I was able to figure it out, I was in my early forties. He never let it show. I gathered most of the pieces from Mom and relatives. Since Dad will be mad at me when finds out I wrote about it, I will leave it at "rough." He escaped the sad times. I think I understand why he turns silent when he is mad. He isn't embarrassed by me. It is just his way of coping, and now I know. Learning about your past and where you fit in is definitely what gives anybody's Vivid Blue some real color.

I have to wonder if my father thinks that schizoaffective equates to something less than admirable. It is the way it is, and I cannot change the facts. I have a disorder, and so do millions of Americans. Sure, I admit, I have a little harder time. I don't discuss my particular psychosis with him. At least, I don't discuss it in any detail. I know my dad still thinks I need to follow the rules. Picking and choosing which rules to adhere to would only lead to a perilous fate. He thinks there is little difference between following social expectations, like holding a door open for a lady, and actual crimes against the law. He expects me to act like a responsible adult. What's more, he wants me to have a conscience, and having a schizoaffective disorder is not an excuse to get away with anything. He will always side with what is right. I work very hard at not letting my disorder affect others. My delusions of paranoia are about people doing things to me. In any case, I can abide by the law because I accept things happening to me. I am not a hostile person. I don't like confrontation, and I shy away from it because any attention makes me feel like "the boy who blew himself up."

There is an incident in my past where I feel certain I was singled out unfairly. I know part of my disorder is feeling paranoia. I didn't know it then, and I am sure over a period of time this behavior got to me. I think there were better ways of handling the situation, but I was young and brash. I didn't know I had a disorder, but that was no excuse. My father and society held me accountable. I think I went overboard in establishing my rights. I was clearly in the wrong, but I was also singled out a little unfairly too. It was a weird situation. I have thought of it often, and I wonder what would have played out differently if I didn't have "the boy who blew himself up" mentality backing me up. I think my paranoia played out in the

107

weirdest way.

The event to which I am referring is the time I ran from a state trooper. You see, at the university where I got my degree, police study to be state troopers. This means (I'm sure, I'm not guessing) they are already law officials. When they start their curriculum, they already have certain powers entrusted to them (that I know). I didn't know it when I was going there, and I am willing to bet most of my classmates didn't either. Heck, some foolhardy guy at school used to call them "fake police," and I was no exception.

One day when my car broke down, I had to borrow my father's old truck. My father had told me that his truck could be used only for school purposes. Because it was a really old truck, having to drive it was an incentive for me to fix my car. I really didn't like that old truck.

My father worked for the government, and he had a contract with UAH. He would not pay for a university decal. If he did, it meant he would get a ticket when he parked the truck in one of his work parking lots. I'm not sure how that worked or even if that was the real reason, but Dad didn't want the decal, and he was willing to pay for the tickets. I know it makes no sense now, and it didn't back then either. The solution was for me to park the truck way out in the "anybody can park here" section and walk a mile to class. I'm not even sure this gray area existed. I didn't want to do this because Dad never used the truck to go to work. It all seemed ridiculous to me. I know why they gave me the tickets, and they should have too. It would have been better for everyone involved if I had just had a decal. I can't make the story short now, but the decal cost X amount. The ticket for not having a decal was X+. The part for the car, which I could not afford, was over eighty dollars. It took me a very long time to fix the car. Before I got the part, I'd accumulated quite a number of tickets. Dad did pay for them. Why he was such a stickler about the part will always puzzle me.

A state trooper had seen the truck in several parking lots, and one day he decided to prove a point. I needed to get a decal. He gave me more than one ticket on the same day. I guess his logic was a ticket for each parking lot. As a matter of fact, it was three tickets that day. I came out of my last class as he was writing the last ticket.

Even though I pointed out this was unfair, he continued to write the ticket. Being the brazen young man that I was, I crumpled up the ticket. He proceeded to write me another ticket. This made me ultra mad. This is the point where I think my disorder was shining through. I was either paranoid that the world was out to get me, or I was a spoiled brat. I bet it was a combination of both.

I immediately hopped in my father's truck, popped the curb, and ran from the state trooper. The whole time I was thinking he was just a fake cop. Since I knew the town, I managed to elude him. He probably didn't want to chase me. The very next day, I got a registered letter stating that I could no longer go to the classes at the university. I told my parents, "It is okay. I just have to go to fake traffic court." My father informed me that it was no "fake traffic court," and that I was in real jeopardy because they were real state troopers.

I had been suspended from the university, and I had to appear before a judge. They were probably going to kick me out of UAH. Hmm. Needless to say, Dad was mad. He was really mad. I was almost dead before the judge even saw me. I really can't remember which was worse! This is where my father started to side with the university. I tried to explain, but it did no good. He wasn't at all swayed by my rationale. He did find it amusing, but he still sided with the school and told me I had better straighten it out or else.

My father and I had a deal. If I dropped out of school, I owed him every penny he had paid for my debts and my tuition. By the time this ticket incident happened, I couldn't afford to quit. Finally I was scared! I appeared before the judge and explained to them that the campus police had given me four tickets (including the one I crumpled) on the same day and that was unfair. I also explained that I had been given quite a number of tickets overall, and I had paid every one of them. The judge was unpersuaded, to say the least. I did make sure to say multiple times that I'd paid all my fines.

My father managed several multimillion-dollar contracts with the university. I thought that his stature as a high-ranking government employee would make a difference, but this fact didn't even sway the judge. The fact that my father did not want a sticker on his truck fell on deaf ears. The judge had to do what was right. He asked me about the decal and was very curious why my father didn't want it on the truck. I told him the decal would mean that he would get a ticket when he parked it at the facility where he held the contract. Basically it was either he gets a ticket or I get a ticket. My father was choosing to let me get the ticket. Besides, I was supposed to walk the mile across the parking lot to avoid all this. The judge, not believing me, told me any father would want a decal on his truck to say that his student went to a prestigious university.

The judge ended up calling my father to find out whether my story was true. Dad came down to the courtroom to straighten it all out. The judge asked my father for the truth, face to face. My father said yes, point blank. The judge asked him, "Would you really pay all that money and not pay for the decal?" My father said yes again. The judge couldn't believe his ears. All I remember correctly is that he let me go. Shaking his head at me, he said (paraphrased), "I cannot believe that you would run from a state trooper." He also said something to the effect of "I honestly cannot believe this whole situation."

The judge turned around my feeling of being singled out unfairly in his ruling. I have to learn not to let my feelings of paranoia get to me. Although it is part of my disorder, I can learn to do better from these life-shaping events. There was a better way of handling the situation. But I was young and brash and I didn't see it at the time. Also, I didn't know I had a disorder then, though that was no excuse. I went overboard in establishing my rights. I was clearly in the wrong, but I was also singled out a little unfairly too. I realized in the end that I had gotten too much attention. I was "the boy who blew himself up," and I didn't want to be singled out again. I didn't do anything like that again the rest of my school career. People do learn from their mistakes, and while schizoaffective disorder remains a constant, the ways in which I handle it can be learned and reinforced.

If I had been lucky enough to have a diagnosis earlier, I could have done things that would have reduced my feeling that the world was out to get me. In my search for a Vivid Blue, I realized life gives us little lessons. My dysfunctionality was really starting to show. My memories are vivid and the lessons are tremendous. My

110

sense of understanding was finally going farther than my nose, and as my grandmother would say, "Bless my pointed little head."

Chapter 18. It Can't Get Any Worse—or Can It?

I know better than to say, "It can't get any worse," because it can. Learning not to say that phrase has been one of the bigger lessons for me as a schizoaffective individual. I sometimes wonder if this isn't my biggest life lesson. It definitely ranks up there at the top. When you suffer from a disorder, you shouldn't tempt fate. Life can always turn south at any moment. If your life is already going south, it might just keep going.

Oscillating between optimism and pessimism is the norm for most schizoaffective bipolar people, and I am no exception. Actually, any of my disorders is a reason to oscillate back and forth. I make wishes when I am at either end of the spectrum, and the middle ground is forever fleeting. In a perfect world, the energy I waste trying to be normal could be channeled into something constructive. I know from my own personal experience that I waste many hours worrying about what to do next. I waste even more time thinking how people might perceive my actions. As a result of my experiences, I have a very bad outlook on the future. Still, I have learned not to say, "It can't get any worse."

My last class at the University of Alabama in Huntsville proved more challenging than any prior courses. I really wasn't as prepared for real-world situations as the university would have preferred. During this course, it got rough, and I actually used the phrase "it can't get any worse." I thought it and I said it more than once during the quarter. You might be thinking that it serves me right. I was building some bad karma, but it should not have mandated complete disaster. Other than that, I would like to think my overall point of view was the same as it is now.

I have some other important philosophies that come in handy when dealing with life. One of the most important is be nice to people and they will be nice in return. We learned this one on the playground in kindergarten. Real adults rarely start fights, but adults do fight, and you will soon understand how it hurts everybody when they do. I need to stress that we saw the signs of my dysfunctionality, but we didn't know what to do about them. I obsessed about this class, and I became the control freak of the group. It didn't save us.

My last senior class was a business policy course. For our class project, we were divided into several groups. Every group included a member with a different major. One had to be in accounting, one had to be in marketing, one had to be in management information systems, and so on. My discipline was management information systems. We all had to work together on our project. Every group's project was on a specific type of business. Our group chose a hospital. The concept was how we would help the business operate more efficiently and be more profitable overall. We had to have a full market strategy. We took turns studying the hospital's operations, and then we made recommendations on our individual part. The presentation was 70 percent of our grade. Unfortunately, during the quarter, our professor got sick. We found out that she had diverticulitis. She wasn't coming back to teach. The business department at that time was small, and there were only two classes on the schedule. There was only one other business policy class that quarter, and it was taught by another professor. We had the option of dropping our class, or he would oversee the course. He would teach us, and then our presentation would be given to the faculty.

Our whole class was disgruntled about giving our presentation to the faculty, but we had to do it to graduate on time. Nobody wanted to drop out. As you might expect, I had the most dysfunctional group in the class. To top it off, I think everybody knew it. There is a force that draws like people together. Still, I was in total denial of my own dysfunction. During my time in class, I met a beautiful girl named Adrian. It didn't take long for her to notice that I was in a dysfunctional group, and I wonder if she somehow knew I was dysfunctional too. She was an inspiration to me, and I couldn't have made it without her. I owe a lot to her pretty smile and her wonderful words of encouragement. She was a godsend.

113

During the quarter, I could not afford the gas to go back and forth between class and home. I was lucky enough to have an hour and a half between my first and second classes. I always went to the library in between the two. This was where our group would meet at the same time every week. Our newly assigned professor would come and check out our study group. I was the only one who consistently showed up. When he noticed everybody's attendance record, I asked if I could break out and do the project on my own. The professor said no, the project "had to be done by everyone." I balked and said this was unfair. He said that rules were rules.

I was in luck in that the new professor had a pretty good sense of humor, though, and I had an idea he would be fair. My big downfall at this time was my midterm grade. I was in a bind and he knew it. He kept telling me to keep on trying. If I had known how dysfunctional the group would be, I would have dropped the class. When it came time for the presentation, everybody was nervous, and I was no exception. I stood up and started the presentation. I knew that I would get scared, and if I didn't start things, it wouldn't go right. You might say I'm a bit of a control freak. Learning to let go is something I have never been able to do. I should have been practicing it then. Anyway, when my part was over and I sat down, that's when all hell broke loose.

Two of our group members stood up at the same time. They started talking at the same time. Then they looked at each other and demanded that they get to speak first. In unison, they started speaking again. Both quit and stared angrily at each other. Then they started talking again at the same time. Finally one of them turned to the other one and screamed, "I was talking!" The other one bobbed her head and looked back and started screaming too.

I was horrified; I couldn't believe this was happening. "Oh, God!" I thought. "Lord, please help me! This can't be happening." My heart pounded. Once again I found myself in a mess. I don't know how I do it, but I always do. They continued to scream at each other. Just then, the faculty stopped us. They lined us up in a row. They asked us what made us think we deserved to graduate. One by one we answered, until they finally got to me.

I said, "I don't know. I've had almost every one of you for

114

my professors." Then I vowed sternly, "I'll be here every single quarter until I graduate!" I started piling papers into my bag. They asked me where I thought I was going. I looked at them and said, "Is there anything I can do to change this outcome?" I remember quite clearly demanding an answer. When they all replied with some form of no, I said, "I'm going home." Just before they let me go, they explained that if this had happened in the real world, we would be going home to our families empty-handed. Our children would starve.

I was very distraught on the drive home. Just outside of class, Adrian stopped me. She was worried about my driving. She was right, of course. I should not have driven home. I almost had an accident, but I did make it home. Once again, I don't handle myself well in bad situations. Again I had been telling myself it couldn't get any worse. This was one of those times I realized I shouldn't tell myself it couldn't get any worse, because it surely could. I got home, sat in my car, and fumed. How could this have happened? Why did adults act like children? I was twenty-eight years old and life had just dealt me a bad card.

I am sure you are asking how it could have gotten any worse. Believe me, it did.

To reach my parents' house, you had to go down a number of steps. From there was a big deck that stretched out nice and wide. I parked at the street. I couldn't bear to go down the steps. It was my last presentation and school was over for me. Well, I desperately wanted to say school was over, but now I couldn't. My parents couldn't wait to hear how it went. I could not stand to face them. I had prepared for this class for four years. It was the class that everybody dreaded, and I was sure to be the subject of the school's newest rumor.

My mother and I were usually on the same page. She could read me like a book. Now she came out to see me, and she knew something was wrong, she just didn't know what. I came down the steps all upset, and believe it or not, I was crying. I knew I wasn't going to graduate. Since I had to tell her, I looked her right in the face and choked out, "I'm not graduating."

"How can that be?" she asked. "You've done so well. This is

your last class." With tears in my eyes, I said emphatically, "I'm not graduating."

Of course, Mom didn't comprehend what I said. So I repeated myself. I stood on the deck trying to get my composure, but I couldn't. At some point my father came out. He put his hand on my mother's shoulder, and he listened to what I was saying. I tried to tell him the story as concisely as I could, but I had to tell him a few times for him to understand me. I felt like the world had done me wrong. Dad said to my mother, "He's not graduating." He knew the ramifications of losing 70 percent of the class grade.

I finally turned to my mom and said, "It cannot get any worse!" I meant what I said too. It was one of those deep-from-the-gut statements that are driven by fear or sadness. Mine was driven by both. I belted it out like the world could hear it. I was standing in front of my parents' house, and I remember it well.

My mother, being the wonderful, sweet, loving lady that she was, looked me right in the eye and said, "Oh no, I just mailed your invitations!" It had just gotten worse! A lot worse! She had just announced to the world that I was graduating. Well, "to the world" is a hyperbole. But she had announced it, that was for sure.

I tend to exaggerate a lot. It is another problem with me. Like when I cleaned out the garage one fall and swept the floor for the termite man. I forgot to close the garage door and took a nap. Afterward, when I looked in the garage, I concluded that every leaf in the neighborhood had blown into my garage. I can't say "all" or "every" without getting into trouble. That is what I was doing when I said "every leaf."

The idea of not graduating made me feel like it had gotten worse, and it was a devastating thing in my world. How on earth was I going to face a sea full of people and tell them I wasn't graduating? "The boy who blew himself up" was going to be center stage once again.

I had to stare adversity in the face, so I promptly did the only thing any young graduating student could do: I crawled in a hole and died, metaphorically speaking. I kept going into my room to hide and came out just to get food. I thought the world had ended. I didn't know how I was going to survive. I couldn't speak to my parents. I couldn't speak to anybody. I didn't know what to do. My grandmother told me I would have to face reality. She kept telling me to go back to the school and see what the professor wanted me to do. I went to the university, and they couldn't tell me what the faculty had decided. The professor had to follow the rules. He said rules were rules, and they were strict. I was tired of hearing that statement. I knew there was nothing I could do. UAH would not break them. I realized that the University of Alabama was a school of principle.

UAH had not broken rules before. Nobody at school was ever caught breaking the rules (except me—I tried and got caught). Lord knows people love to succeed in catching me. They were not going to break the rules now, not for my last class and not at the last moment. They were not going to break the rules, period. That's when I realized that I was facing certain adversity. But as I walked out of the office, the professor said to me, "I do love the way you threatened the faculty."

"What?" I said.

"Yes, we took what you said as a threat."

I turned around, looked him straight in the eye, and said, "I did not."

"Don't you remember you threatened the faculty?"

"I did not."

"You did," he insisted. "You said you'd be here every single quarter until you got your degree, and we take that as a threat." Then he laughed and winked at me.

When the grades came out, I got a 70, barely a C. It was just enough to pass the class. There was one other person who graduated with me; she had gotten a higher grade on the midterm. Nobody else passed without some summer classes, and the ones who had started the fight failed. With God's help, I graduated with my class of '93. My GPA wasn't the best, but it was sufficient.

I had the promise of a new career and a new life because of graduating. I also had my disorders, and they would follow me to my career. I can only help the ones who want to read my words and absorb what I am saying. It is never too late to start fixing your life. Yes, I have many bad moments. Yes, I have my disorders and suffer

117

from them, immensely. I get baited into bad actions, and I need to pay attention to my own words. But there are times when I am on the right track, and those times are getting longer and more frequent. I have more encouragement, and when I look beyond my nose, I realize there are more people in the world who want me to get better. The good people outweigh the bad. This is the gist of my book and what I am writing about. It is so vivid.

Chapter 19. My New Career

I graduated UAH in the class of 1993. My overall GPA wasn't very high. I like to think I purposely sacrificed the grades to get out of school faster. The real truth had more to do with the fact that it was a very tough school, and I was scattered in my thoughts. I did step up the pace at the end, but not nearly enough to make a great difference. As for the grades, part of my rationale was that I already had mediocre grades from my freshman year, so I didn't need to keep a great average. I felt positive I could redeem myself on the first job. I think my OCD kept me trying, and the professors saw my intentions as genuine. I also think I was able to hide all other problems because I was an expert at being a recluse. Still, I know I deserved to graduate because I did the work just like everybody else and proved I could do it.

Again, I can't be objective about my bipolar behavior, but it was becoming closer to the time I was diagnosed. After all, I graduated at twenty-eight and my first diagnosis was at 32. I am glad I spent the effort to get my degree because it is one of the few things in life that can't be taken away. Take it from a person diagnosed with schizoaffective disorder, a degree is priceless. I am not sure how much it helps in the work world, though, because the amount of time you spend with your work mates will illuminate your problems, but having a degree helps your self-esteem. It also helps give a foundation of skills that are taken for granted, like writing, finance, and general business. With all the medicine I am ingesting, a part of me wonders if I could do it again. At a minimum, I have memory issues. It was a very tough school, but I am not surprised I made it. I will make one concession: the latest medicine, Abilify, has made a positive difference.

After I got my degree, I didn't look for a job in Huntsville because I was tired of the whole scene. My father thought I should be working at the local research park, but if I found a job in the next few months, he wouldn't say anything. He knew I wanted to live in Atlanta. He was open-minded about my efforts, but if I didn't find a job by the end of summer, he said I had to come home and look. I don't think I gave it my all, and I wound up home looking for a job.

I managed to find a job after the summer of my graduating year. It was roughly five months after the job I'd had during my senior year fizzled. That the job fizzled was no fault of my own. The owner of the company sold out to SAIC, and I was one of the employees who didn't get picked up on the new contract. I was a temporary employee, and that's the way contract life goes. I found another job at a very large contractor.

I learned a valuable lesson from this new corporation. I learned I could be obnoxious. I was obnoxious because I went out and proved I was worth something. For most of my life, I had deep-seated feelings about throwing the spray can into the fire. After I got this new job, I unleashed a monster. I never knew how obnoxious I was before all this, and now I doubled it. It didn't matter to anybody that most of it was a defense mechanism. People saw it and didn't like it. I'm ashamed of it too. I acted just as badly as the people I was condemning. There was one problem. They had obvious reasons for their bad behavior. They had too much money to care about the little people. I needed to put myself in check before I became an evil monster. I didn't have the same excuses, and people weren't going to give me any outs.

I have learned that obnoxiousness runs in my family like a brook through a forest. My personal obnoxiousness was more like a flash flood through a gorge after a heavy rain in the Colorado mountains. Many members of my extended family are better at hiding their problems. We have a unique way of handling each other too—we bicker. Anyway, all my family have learned the art of ducking, dodging, and verbally attacking. They learned these skills from each other. Every relative has become an artisan of verbal warfare. Sharp-clawed, deep wounds would result, and nobody would go unscarred. We all became a motley crew, and I am sad to say that I had many a bad day when I was to blame for starting it. My artillery mouth was fully engaged in attack or defense. It makes no difference how you justify it when you are hurt or need help. It has only gotten better because we grew up and some moved away. But that is where most of my obnoxiousness comes from. The other is insecurity stemming from burn-related trauma. It shouldn't have carried over to the work world, but it carried over everywhere.

During the mornings and afternoons, I used to get a big kick out of driving to and from work. I thought it was a big deal. That wears off faster than the smell of a new car, though. What doesn't wear off is the luxury of working in an office. I felt lucky to be working at our local research park. I loved it. I started to move around the office like I lived there, making myself useful in any way possible. Well, my OCD made me feel useful. I have always been the type to stay busy (until I became depressed), because watching the clock makes the day longer than any unpleasant assignment. I fancied myself as a programmer, but I still had a lot to learn. I was getting on-the-job training.

The days were long, but I was already used to that. I never gave myself time to think, because if I did, I would cyclically think there was a problem. It was a good time to be OCD. Well, there never is a good time to be OCD. I must have had a world of other problems too. After I had been on the project for a while, they pulled me off the programming side. It was because I wasn't getting along with one of the programmers. He said I wasn't blending my code with his, and he had to write his code around mine. It was making more work for him. Since he had more seniority and was a much better coder, they reassigned me. It was very unfair. I was never going to become a better programmer. Looking back on it, I wonder how much my schizoaffective disorder had to do with it. The OCD was there. If they'd told me in time, I would have spent hours to correct my coding.

I choose not to overanalyze the past because it only hurts my self-esteem. There are parts that did not work out very well, and I shouldn't focus on those. My work was good enough for them to assign the whole help file to me. This was no small task, and there were quite a few things that needed to be done to link into each screen. It wasn't like it is today, where all you need to do is worry about the content.

During the time I was making the help file, I had the fortune of working for a judiciously fair man by the name of Mickey. His wife was going through the ordeal of cancer. As anybody knows, cancer is a horrible disease. Also working for Mickey was my direct boss, Kurt, who presided over our team. On our team was a lady who didn't like me, but she seemed to be the only one. There were others who didn't get along with her, but they didn't butt heads with her like I did. Go figure. It was probably because of my disorders. It was not because I was lazy or incompetent. Again, there was a higher probability of her not liking me because I was dysfunctional. I will take the time to say that she did have one girl fired, but there was a rumor that the girl wasn't very good at her job. I think everybody who worked there was scared.

When I first got the help file assignment, I was hurt because I wanted to be a programmer. It didn't register with me that I was the only one given this task and that there was a lot of responsibility. I was good at seeing only what I wanted to see, and to me it was a demotion. My boss, Kurt, had to give me a pep talk when he gave me the assignment. He even had to tell me he had faith in my ability. I took it on with great contempt, but then I started to like what I was doing. I realized how many intricate parts of the program needed to be explained to the user. Not only was it a large endeavor, it required knowing the whole program from top to bottom. I had to test every possible way a user could enter the help screen and then accommodate their wanting to do a multitude of things. I did all this with yesteryear software. It really was a lot. I did, however, have the use of a tech writer, and she was great. We shared an office, and my only complaint was she played Tom Petty every day. I mean every day, way beyond my OCD.

Kurt told me that the team leader would be the lady who didn't like me. I didn't notice anything out of the ordinary at first because she either hid her feelings or they built over time. After some time, though, her animosity toward me grew. Early on in the project, I made a few connections to each screen and did the write-ups. It was just for a test. Then it would be easy to move on to each new part of the program. It started to happen: she started having me correct things. It was a few minor things at first, but by the time it was over, she told Kurt that I was missing deadlines. Then she claimed I was not turning in very good work. It turned into a real mess. I had worked on a previous contract with the company, and they had no problem except they needed to give me the corner cubicle because I was feeling paranoid. But that was a different story.

Anyway, I was made to do each screen over and over. I kept telling Kurt that it had already been done, or that it couldn't be done to her satisfaction. I was made to do it in so many ways that it was getting redundant. I was told that this wasn't right and that wasn't right until I had to put it back to the way I originally had it. Finally she went over Kurt's head and stormed into Mickey's office. She screamed, "This is the kind of work Mark does!" She acted like she hated me, that I am sure.

I was scared, but I had kept a paper trail, as my father had advised me to do. Thank God I finally took his advice. My document was all scratched up in red! It looked like a first grader had somehow made a college exam. I was horrified! Mickey called me into his office and said to me, "We don't have time for this, Mark. Take this and justify all these red marks."

I couldn't believe it. She was trying to get me fired. I said, "I will need the rest of the day." Well, I took my paper trail and showed Mickey that she had me go back and forth so many times that it was redundant. I said that I was being run around. I finally ended up justifying all the marks. I tried not to be snotty when I said, "Some of my grammar issues were results of her re-writes" To her dismay, it wasn't me who got fired that day. I did work out that contract, and I got picked up on the next contract. That is how I ended up at the Corps of Engineers.

I could remain angry about the events that transpired, or I could have allowed myself to become bitter. That would be counterproductive. I heard a saying one time and I like to think I follow it. It goes, "You either grow sour, or you grow sweet." Well, I refuse to let the events in my life make me sour. I want to remain a fresh soul with lots to give. The search for a Vivid Blue has proven to be a challenging road, and one that needs quite a bit of work to hone. Undoing all the negative energy that comes my way takes everything I have, but when I succeed, the rewards are immeasurable.

Chapter 20. Developing a Catlike Confidence

Living with yourself and your disorders requires more wisdom than I am personally able to convey. I don't have the answers for myself, and I haven't done a very good job of mapping them out so I could logically tackle them. That is partially the reason behind the concept for my Vivid Blue. I want to change the direction or course. I want to plan my next move. I want to know why I do the things that make me schizoaffective, OCD, and whatever. It is important to me that I stop falling into the same ruts and get moving along with my life. Among all of God's creatures, the cat is the one I would like to emulate. Cats show a mastery of nature and a sleek confidence that I find very refreshing. My next story illuminates a confidence that any person knowingly battling a plight can gather some insight. Basically, you can laugh at yourself in your most embarrassing moments. It won't make you less of a person to acknowledge your vulnerabilities. I had to see this behavior in somebody else before I could apply it to my life. If only it were instinctual. But I learned that with a quick reversal of programmed thoughts, I could manage it. I already managed to control my anger. Imagine what else might be possible if we try.

I heard it said once that the voice is the first thing you forget when a loved one passes. I'm not entirely sure that is true. As a matter of fact, I seriously doubt it. If that is the case, then I must be different. I will tell you that I can still hear the laughter of my best friend bellowing in one of our best times. It reverberated in the enclosed area, and you couldn't help but notice the deep richness carrying through it with a raspy, sheepish, childlike innocence. My friend wasn't innocent at all, we had just caught him in a funny moment, and he too was laughing at himself. Luckily for us, he wasn't the type to get defensive or bent out of shape. He just went with the flow and had the catlike confidence to which I am referring. It didn't faze him a bit that we were laughing so hard we couldn't see straight. He just laughed too.

My friend Scott had an uncanny ability to put insecurity in its place. Sure, he was human, and it did bother him when he was pressured, but he handled himself better than most. I, on the other hand, had a lot to learn. Funny thing, I knew he could show me the ropes if I listened. We had a symbiotic relationship. After all, isn't that what friendship is about? You look to your friends for inspiration, and hopefully they will possess the qualities that can inspire you to move mountains. I learned a lot that day, but I never knew it until many years later.

We woke up one particular morning not knowing what we were going to do with the rest of the day. The day itself wasn't memorable; it wasn't as though it were raining or anything like. We had a lazy day to fill our insatiable need for a good time. Scott had just moved to Atlanta and I was visiting him. It was a big change from our hometown, and we were enjoying every little opportunity we could. It showed how green we still were to big-city life. We had a full day to do anything we chose, and the city seemed to be our oyster. What were we going to do? Well, first things first. We would get brunch at a cool new restaurant or establishment. Scott was keeping his ear to the ground, and there was always a new one he wanted to try. After all, it was his thing. He had a social thing going and loved the ambiance of a new environment. Chatting up the server or patron was like butter to him. He knew all the right words to say and spoke with ease. He was fluent in body language as well.

During our morning meal, we decided to go to the Atlanta Zoo. It seemed to be one more thing to cross off our Atlanta bucket list, and it would occupy the day with a minimum drain on the pocketbook. Never did I think it would be such a memorable experience. The entrance was uneventful because it was generic; I don't remember a thing about it. As a matter of fact, all I remember is walking around a lot and looking at most of the sights. That is until it happened. You know how memories are—everything before and after is a blur, but the event is always with you. And so it goes…

We might as well have been at a circus for some of the events, but the one that wins the prize was the lion's den. Over the years, I've found great joy in thinking about the setting because of my fondness for the feline species. The only way the story could be any better is if I were describing white tigers, but alas, I must let the story stand on its own merit. Anyway, in the middle of our adventure, we stood outside the lion's den thinking about what exhibits we would visit next, and in which order. We chose the lion's den because it was the closest. Technically it was just behind us, and we would start there after our mapping was done.

There were two entrances, or maybe an entrance and an exit when the zoo was really crowded. This particular day we were lucky. The zoo was practically empty, and we had the place to ourselves—well, almost. When you entered the den, it took time for your eyes to adjust, but when they did, you could see everything. It was a cave-like room with large windows that looked out upon the lion's den. As you walked in from either side, you looked through the glass as though it were an aquarium. You then spied on the lions with no possible way of being detected, because it was one-way glass. It was a way of keeping the lions from getting perturbed or restless. The concept worked very well because the interaction with the animals was kept nonexistent.

Out of the corner of my eye, I could see the room's two entrances. Then a lady entered with a small child. She brought him to the window next to ours. She pointed and said to her child, "That's a lion." The young child got excited and they watched some more, ultimately moving back to some benches in the middle of the room. They were large stationary benches with no backs. The lady pulled out some candy or treats for the child, and they just watched the lions.

That was when Scott got the idea to sit, but the bench was taken. He saw a chair off to the side and decided to enjoy the lions himself, and he wanted to sit and casually absorb the show. He walked over, grabbed the edge of the chair, and pulled it across the room. As the chair moved across the room, it made a rich dragging sound. It rumbled from the friction and echoed in the room with a coarse sound. It was an obvious sound to me and very apparent to the lady sitting on the bench. At the same moment, by nature's practical joke, the biggest lion in the den opened his mouth and yawned. It was a great big yawn too, and it looked like the lion had roared.

Scott immediately stopped dragging the chair and ran up to

the window. He exclaimed, "Did you hear that? The lion roared!" Without being cognizant of his actions, and not knowing that it had been the chair, he looked at me for some sort of confirmation.

"No, Scott, it's the chair," I said.

Then he got even more excited and said, "Maybe he will do it again!" He turned to the lady and the kid and said, "Did you hear that?" and then he looked right at me and said, "They must be piping in the sound."

I started giggling. "It was the chair!" I said again. Still he was sure he had just heard a lion roar. He was elated, and I was too, but for a different reason. I couldn't help it, I kept giggling. I looked over at the lady, and we started to laugh together. I said to Scott, "If it were piped-in sound, then where are the speakers?"

Unfortunately for Scott, that was the moment he realized there were no speakers. Then he had the moment we all face when we realize we have spotlighted ourselves. He had two choices—to laugh or to be defensive. He chose to hold his composure perfectly, laugh, and not even make excuses like most people would. In one second he handled himself in a way I only hope to achieve in my next moment in the spotlight.

Scott turned the moment around. He ended up introducing himself to the lady and chatting up a storm. I remember that day fondly and will tell the story to anyone who will listen. I certainly will point out how refreshing it is to have a catlike confidence and to be able to laugh at something and not feel burdened by the weight of insecurity. My search for a Vivid Blue will always remind me to look to the constants in life that teach us more by example. In this case, both cats and Scott were shining examples of how to behave in any situation. I managed to utilize a little of that when it was accidentally illuminated in a conversation that I was schizophrenic. The way in which it came about was in reference to a study on mental illness, and they were just trying to inform me of a new treatment that might interest me. In this conversation, you could tell that people were taken aback by the information gathered. The person who mentioned it didn't know what had transpired or he certainly would have chosen different words or a different time to tell me. He said there was a new study on schizophrenia and then

127

basically directed the conversation at me. All eyes were on me, and I could only acknowledge the statement and move forward with the conversation. I didn't change the course of the conversation, and I just agreed with the initial topic. I hoped that I handled it like my buddy's shining example. Owning up to our plight is something we do on a constant basis, and even though we might be taught how to deal with it, it doesn't make the event any easier. I actually think there are moments where people will slip up faster than I will, so I have to just come out and put the cards on the table. I realized I didn't have to walk on eggshells. How an SABP person—heck, a mentally ill person—handles the situation almost always feels wrong. The search for a Vivid Blue has taught me to draw from a deep well of people who are not alone in this and to look toward people who inspire me with ways to handle it.

Chapter 21. The Hole in My Heart

My dear friend Scott was murdered on December 17, 1996, in Atlanta. I was in Huntsville at the time, so who knows what really went on when it happened. Scott's death was so personal to me that I get excruciatingly sad when thinking about it. It was a horrendous murder with a long trial, so I just can't get into specifics. Someday I might write a little something more on the trial, but for now it will remain untouched by my pen. I will say that the person responsible is serving time, and his lousy story about it not being premeditated didn't hold water in court. I do, however, forgive the person who committed the crime. It is what Scott would have wanted.

Scott was the type of friend who encourages one to do better. I used to ask him why we were friends, and he would tell me, "Because you are a Mark Original." He was one of the most instrumental characters in my life. I have to use the word "instrumental" to describe him because music was his passion. He had a degree in computer science and a minor in music from the University of Alabama. His mother told me that he had enough credit hours for three degrees. I was different. I started out with a few too many problems. I used to tell my parents I could be successful without a degree. I conned myself into believing it didn't matter, because I wanted to be in business for myself. In the past I had been a paperboy, managed a video store, and opened a tool and equipment rental store. I ended up getting a degree after all was said and done. I don't know what I would have done without Scott's peppy little witticisms, and without him, his mother and John would not be part of my family. Sue, Scott's mom, is an inspiration, and John is without a doubt the most delightful…how I should put this?…elevated spirit I have ever known.

John is a librarian, like my grandmother was. It is no wonder word games come easier for me than other games. My father told me that I was horrible at math and needed to choose a career that wouldn't require higher mathematics. Originally I wanted to be an architect. I wanted to build a home of my own and make it all that ours wasn't. Although I was gifted with imagination and dreams, when paper met concrete, I could forget it. Scott had a computer science degree and could work the numbers easily. He used to take a grocery receipt and figure out everybody's share without a calculator. He'd added up the individual items we all picked up along the way. My grandmother and my father were the only other people I knew who could do this type of mathematical wizardry.

Wizardry didn't help Scott through his roughest time. He always saw the best in people and would have given you the shirt off his back. I sometimes wonder if that was the very reason he found himself in the casket. There is no sense in glossing it over. He didn't deserve what happened to him. Nothing can change it, and I will always wonder if I had been in Atlanta like I had planned, would things have been different? Sadness creeps into my soul, and I know his mother suffers every day.

I remember how my grandmother cried in the phone message telling me I needed to call her. I never imagined it being Scott's death. I thought something terrible had happened in my life, not in his. I called my grandmother and she cried. I thought to myself, "What could it be?" She cried and cried. She finally uttered the words, "I can't tell you. You have to call your parents." Well, I immediately knew that it wasn't my parents, so it must be my uncle. Our family was so prone to strokes. Heck, everybody in my family has had strokes for generations. We have been riddled with the horrible plight, one after the other, for years.

I called my parents and asked what was wrong. My mother instructed me to call Scott house. She probably assumed that grandma told me the dreadful news. I called Scott's house and erroneously said, "Let me speak to Scott." It was the worst thing in the world to say. His mom's best friend answered. I remembered her because Scott asked me to deliver her flowers one time and pretend I was a delivery boy. We would always try to save money like that. Anyway, she was puzzled.

"Who is this?" she asked politely but sternly.

"It's Mark. Let me speak to Scott."

There was a long pause and then she said, "Hold just a moment."

Sue, Scott's mom, got on the phone. "Mark, I am sorry to tell you Scott's dead."

I couldn't believe my ears. For the first time, I went to my knees.

Sue was a lady of such good character. She took the bull by the horns! She faced everything with the grace of God. She later explained to me that Scott's favorite spiritual song was "Cornerstone," and she gave me a tape of it. It took me a long time to listen to that song. I haven't even opened the original yet, the one she gave me because she thought I didn't have Scott's. I have her writing on the original and I want to keep it.

The night before Scott died, I told my grandmother I was selling my house. It was the house she'd helped me buy with her gift of a down payment. That very night, I had taken all my friends to my favorite restaurant and told them I was moving to Atlanta. I had just taken three weeks off from work to look for a job. It was a Tuesday, December 17. We buried Scott that Friday. He was supposed to come home that day for Christmas. Sadness! How could sadness be a part of my search?

When Sue first told me that Scott was dead, I kept thinking there must be many variations of his full name, at least several named with two *s*'s or one *t*, or many other possibilities. Many other things ran through my mind as a dear friend drove me to Scott's mom's house because I couldn't think. I get very emotional and irrational when I know there is something wrong. I always know when there is something wrong. God gave me that ability and it is a gift. I can't tune it. It doesn't help that I run around frantically, and that scares the bejesus out of me. Lord knows I have wandered and found the light, so to speak.

I finally got there, and the whole family was there to greet me, dressed impeccably. They always dressed nicely, and it was Scott's signature series. It was one of those things that I wished had carried over to me. It did in a way, because it was Scott who kept me from looking like a slob. I learned to lose a hundred pounds of depression weight I had gained during college by Scott telling me I could do it. I keep it off now because of him. I still hear him tell me, "Straighten your collar" or "You can't go out like that." You see,

131

Scott was the best-dressed person I knew. He loved to dress me, and then he would get mad when everybody noticed me. I didn't want the attention. I was the "the boy who blew himself up." Scott used to say, "I have the brains. You have the brawn. Let's make lots of money." It was from a song by the Pet Shop Boys. This was just one of many of our favorite tunes. Fact was, secretly I used to chase success. So much so, I would crab at Scott when he gave a dollar to every homeless person he saw. He was very generous with his modest waiter's salary.

It's kind of ironic: my brother just complained the other day because I gave some money to a homeless guy. He said, "If I you're borrowing from Dad and giving money to beggars, you're just giving away Dad's money."

I laughed and said, "You don't have a job, and Dad should have dumped his loads of heavy baggage a long time ago. No wonder Dad is nuts. What is our excuse?" I thank God my dad has as much character as Grandma did.

I was thirty-two years old when Scott was shot and I was first diagnosed with bipolar disorder. I must admit, I had never even heard the term then. I went into the doctor's office for depression because I couldn't cope. I thought I would talk to a therapist and possibly take some pills to help me through the bad spell. I ended up eighteen years later getting a diagnosis of schizoaffective disorder, OCD, and PTSD. The time has been agonizing and long. How could I possibly have this bad of a problem when it was my friend who was shot? How could I need a plethora of pills designed to make me stable when I thought I was only depressed? Eighteen years later, I have more questions than answers, and no place to find solutions. There are no words to explain how I feel or to answer the questions I have concerning my illness.

How did I make it through my teens and my twenties? It makes no sense. I look back and think, "I was lucky to have so much energy." I certainly don't have that energy now. I feel drained. Is this what the doctors intended? I have to believe they are right. I have to believe that my medicines are working like they should. It is not a laughing matter, yet it has to be comical. The first wave of medicines didn't work, or it was my fault for quitting. I look at the second wave of medicines and realize that I have to take them or there will be a third wave. There is no room for feelings where my medications are concerned. If I were to go by feelings, I would resort to not wanting to take any medicines at all. Falling prey to this sort of thought process just leads to trouble. In fact, my parents were so sure of this that they made me a promise: they would pay for my medicines if I promised to take them. I have accepted their generosity for so long, it would be an unforgivable action to betray them at this point. I hate taking my meds, but I do it.

I go back to the age-old question: Where do I go from here? I can always answer the question with another question. Again, where does that lead me? I have a mélange of answers to each question. There are a plethora of questions. I have used that phrase before, and I will use it again and again before the nightmare is over. My search is taking me full circle. I need to analyze things like honesty, truth, and courage in order to understand it all. Once again, the memory of loved ones is the most crucial part of my search and will always be the most vivid. Vivid Blue is about coming to grips with all the things that happen in a person's life. Just because an event is vividly blue, like the death of your best friend, doesn't mean you should give up. Scott wouldn't have given up. I try not to disappoint him. So for me, the day I came to grips with my life was a good day. The sadness is bitter, but the knowledge that I am stronger is what holds me together.

Chapter 22. Knowing What You're Dealing With

Since this book is supposed to be mainly about my schizoaffective disorder, I had better get started discussing the pesky little details. I've spent way too much time explaining my formative problems. This book isn't supposed to be a whine story about my life. It sure did turn out to be quite the saga of "the boy who blew himself up" and other sordid mishaps. By now you have a judgment, and I can't do anything to change that. The best I can hope for is to try to explain what has helped me find some peace with most of my issues. It is my hope that this book will be written in a way that the reader can absorb what has happened and not let it happen to them. Since most of my problems were a direct result of my disorders and actions, I am trying to lay it on the line. I have to assume I am really schizoaffective and therefore try to write in a way that people will understand. I must, repeat must, write with a balanced outlook.

What I am really concerned with is conveying my feelings and letting others (family members and friends too) know that there is light at the end of the tunnel. It doesn't have to be looked at like it is a train, either. I hit bottom in summer of 2011, and I really thought it was the worst time in my life. I also thought people were wishing bad things upon me, or I thought they were bragging about their perfect lives when mine was falling apart. My perceptions, right or wrong, were useless in my personal efforts toward better health and a better life. I needed to focus on my circumstances and what I could do about them. Most of all, I needed to forget where anybody fell into that equation. For a paranoid schizoaffective, it was seemingly impossible, but I did it. I soon became a master at forgetting that there were people out there, and it helped me fix my little world.

It's sad that I had to alienate the people who were trying to help, but it couldn't work any other way. My problems weren't theirs, and therefore they couldn't solve them. As a matter of fact, looking to others sometimes made it worse. I won't go into specifics, but I am quite sure a problem must be solved by the person facing the dilemma. Yes, you can get help with external forces like money, cars, clothes, and medications. Also, you soon figure out who is willing to help and who will run for the hills. Be that as it may, my inability to think clearly when faced with my schizoid behavior was a curse, and even family whom I trusted weren't helping. I looked for little confirmation statements that would undermine any advancement in my treatment. My father would say things like "You're on that kick again," or my brother would say a snippy little "You have it easy." My favorite was "You're just like Mom," as if to suggest I inherited it. It was a way of both trying to get me to improve and blaming me for my behavior. Some of this was at Mom's physical/mental expense, for lack of better terminology.

I even considered my precarious financial situation as mental torture. I obsessed about losing my good salary at the same time I obsessed over paying the bills. To top that off, there was the outright humiliation of asking my parents for money when I should have been thankful for 1) having parents to borrow from, and 2) having parents who were willing and had a little extra to lend. My whole perspective was so out of whack, and I was worried about what I deemed "the hell" of my schizoaffective disorder. I raged like a bull in a china shop. I did all sorts of things to get attention, and in retrospect I don't know how I or anybody who loved me survived. We just did.

I know I am supposed to have wonderful words of wisdom, and I am supposed to say something here that is completely reassuring so that people will take my words to the bank. I know I am supposed to make people believe all their disorders will eventually work out with time and the right medicine. For the most part, it did work that way for me. There is one exception, though: I am still paranoid. I still think thoughts I have to squelch. I am in no way near the point of meltdown like I was in 2011. I think I will be fine. I also think tomorrow will work out, somehow. It goes with the faith that the medicine is working like it should. I don't think answers come for all the people who pray, and maybe not even for all the people who do everything right. Why it is that some people respond to treatment and others don't? I ask the bigger question:

Why is it that some people suffer mental illness, while others are blessed with normal lives? For both, I have no answers, and I know better than to ask somebody else for their opinion. I can say this: it will always leave room for simple minds to discriminate or unjustly make false assumptions.

I don't want to make general statements about groups of people, because I don't want simple-minded people making general statements about a group of schizoaffective people. Typically, they might accidentally get it right, but there we go again, making somebody feel bad by classifying them as bad beforehand. It almost assuredly gives somebody with a diagnosis a reason to hang his head rather than to walk proud. I am quite aware that I am just as good as anybody else, and some of my actions in certain areas need to be in check, but in areas that require compassion, they are on the mark.

You cannot police the world, and you shouldn't try. That is a laughable statement, isn't it? Nobody ever said the world would be fair. I get into this argument every other weekend with a good friend of mine. He has repeatedly said, "Fair should be removed from the dictionary." We all know what context he means; he says it in response all the people he thinks want to live "off the system" or "want a free ride." He will admit there is a need for social services, but he focuses on the corrupt individuals and says the whole country has gone to s***. He will then say our country's ethics are in question. I, on the other hand, focus the other way, on helping the ones in need. We probably both go to extremes. I cannot solve it in this book, and the only reason to bring it up is to say that the important thing is to remember is that every family is affected by mental illness, if not directly, then by association. What's more, it's worse if you are ignorant and can't identify it for what it really is and subsequently choose a proper course for dealing with it.

I'm not outright calling anybody ignorant. I am just stating a fact. If you don't know what you are dealing with, there is a good chance you will make it worse. For example, when they treated my mother for hoarding in the early years, they didn't know the things they do now. They also weren't faced with paralyzing statistics. The success rates are what they are, and saying things like "The person has to want to get help" is flabbergasting to me. I have heard them all. When I talk about how I have dealt with it, I have heard statements like "Imagine how much it affected her." I got mixed messages like it was my fault for "enabling" it, but then out of the other side of their mouths they'd say, "But you were so young when it started."

The one story that really fries my potato happened when I was much younger. We (meaning our whole extended family) decided to do an intervention. It was our intention to "help" Mom see her way past her disorder by removing her from her house. Wow, I'm not even sure that sounds correct, unless a hoarder is trying to hurt himself, and Mom wasn't. We blindsided her at Grandma's house and didn't even give her time to go home and change clothes. I hated every minute of it. Everybody else was doing a great job of convincing everybody the doctor was right. We had a multitude of reasons for why it had to be done. It seemed logical that this was the only way to clean the house of what everybody deemed "her mess." Dad and Lance took the ball and ran with it, while I said I would have no part in it. I guess I was considered the "great enabler." Nobody accused me of anything, they just left me alone. I, being the youngest, had no answers, and yes, I was a momma's boy. Thirty years later we will still argue about my culpability, probably wholeheartedly once this book is published. I distinctly remember not loading up Dad's truck.

When we went to the hospital to visit Mom, it was sheer torture. She looked like a beaten horse. She wasn't the mom I remembered from my youth. She wasn't feisty, cheerful, or anything the like. The hospital certainly wasn't Club Med or a retreat of any kind. I used to make up all sorts of stories about this event, but it is time I came clean. It was probably her worst day. Since, it was my parents' biggest fight of all time, it definitely won out over a specific reason for divorce. I am sure she felt betrayed, but she couldn't isolate it to just my father. She had her mother, aunt, and children to thank for her hell, all because she wanted books and magazines, and that was deemed a "disorder." It was, of course, but wow, she wasn't hurting herself, and geez, I still don't know if it was the right thing to do. What would have really worked? This was just as traumatic an event for the family as it is for the hoarder.

That is all beside the point. The first day or second at the hospital, Mom was ushered away from us and we were told that visiting hours were over. I, feeling very bad and quite regretful, wished there was something I could do. It was never my intention to take every book and magazine away from her. Unbeknownst to me, it must have been the doctors who suggested it.

I asked the doctor, who will remain nameless, if we could give her an *Architectural Digest* or *National Geographic*. They were her favorites. "It goes like this," he said. "A camel and his master are walking through the desert, and it gets dark. The master pitched a tent and prepared for a long, cold night. It wasn't long before it got cold, and the master sealed himself up in the tent to keep the winds out. Just then he heard a knock, and the camel said, 'Can I please stick my head in to keep my ears from freezing? I sure would like to breathe some warm air.' This was acceptable to the master, so he opened the tent just a little and let the camel put his head inside. This went on for a few hours, and everybody was happy until the camel started to complain that he was uncomfortable. The way he was standing hurt, and his feet were cold. He said to the master, 'Could I just put my front two feet in the tent? I would be more comfortable. You have a big tent, and it is very cold out here.' The master, being a softie, agreed and let the camel move farther into the tent." Then the doctor got a little abrupt. "Once the camel had his foot in the door, it didn't take long for the whole camel to enter and the tent didn't work anymore."

"Now" he said snottily, "what do you think?"

I was pissed. Actually, I was beyond pissed. The doctor couldn't have pushed a bigger red button. My aunt knew it too. I told him he hadn't given me a straight answer, and never again would he talk to me as though I were a child. He said no and walked away. I have never run across anybody since who has made me that angry. He must revel in his ignorance or lack of ability to deal with adults. I have run across many doctors who have used the storytelling tactic to explain life situations; it must be common practice in dealing with children and simple folk like me. Well, I really haven't figured out why some doctors use a parable, but very few use them as well as a good writer uses metaphors. Still, I don't let people make me that mad. I use that as an example of my ability to master the situation. Even if I hadn't come up with the right things to say to him, I could choose to diffuse his arrogance without it affecting me.

Unfortunately, I could do nothing about the power he wielded, and it was my opinion that that power had been granted by sheer mistake. If the intervention was necessary and the right thing to do, we most definitely had the worst doctor. This backs up my point that knowing what you're dealing with is crucial to helping both the patient and his or her family members.

I don't want to beat this drum to death, but it is what the chapter is about: knowing what you're dealing with. And that takes time and probably—I don't say it lightly—a maximum number of resources. My problems weren't identified until I was in my mid-to-late forties, and we started the process when I was in my early thirties. We went through times when I had no insurance and my mother was paying the bills out of pocket, and we went through times when I thought I wasn't bipolar and didn't need my meds. It was a long process. It is still one that needs honing, and adjustments will always be necessary. It will be easier for everyone if we all look at it for what it is and not just an isolated event or symptom. I don't look at the future as scary or as ideal. I really don't think about the future, other than to plan for things that I think I might be able to control. I think about retirement, but I don't give up the slice of life that is the here and now. Tomorrow might be too far away. I do what I can, and if I need to do more, I will try to do better on the next go-round.

This turned out to be a longer chapter than I originally intended. I think knowing what you are dealing with is important, and after backing up my point, who doesn't? I also think the search for a Vivid Blue is all about putting the pieces together with that goal in mind. If you're new to the problem and things don't make sense, give it time and don't do anything drastic. If you have time under your belt and things still don't make sense, you're not alone. I don't understand everything about my predicament, but I do know the constants.

Chapter 23. Where My Paranoia May Have Started

When I first realized there were bad memories popping into my head, I asked my brother, "Why didn't you tell Mom about that time? Why didn't you tell Mom that girl got me naked?" It was like I had been expecting my older brother to protect me. The girl who got me naked was maybe four or five years older than I when it started, and I couldn't have been more than eight or nine myself. The girl lived directly across the street, and she managed to get me undressed on many occasions. I couldn't believe I had repressed these experiences. I had buried them so deep that they didn't surface until I was almost forty. My childhood friend might have molested me. Well, molested is probably too strong a term for it. I was a curious child.

The definition of molestation is quite diverse, but I think it is basically taking advantage of somebody sexually. We were all so young when I lived in my first neighborhood. She was barely thirteen or fourteen. Like I mentioned, I couldn't have been more than eight or nine. Maybe I am a little off in my age, but I was too young for sex. When the sexual light comes on, so to speak, you know. I know my light wasn't on. It would take a few more years for me to start working sexually. From what I have learned, I was a late bloomer. I have heard recently that kids as young as six were fooling around. Where does that leave me?

The only relevance to my story is this is the first time I remember being watched. I have to put all feelings in context of that moment. Sometimes it makes me want to retreat. I like being somebody's focus, because I never seem to get enough attention. Well, not watched. This is in direct conflict with "the boy who blew himself up." I am becoming more callous, and dealing with things is getting easier with the right medicine. As before, management is what you do after your diagnosis. Until then, all you do is cope. I coped for many years, because I never even remembered being undressed or even watched.

Upon confronting my brother about those times, he responded with less than the expected compassion. "You mean *all* those times?" he retorted. "I was jealous." He also said quite hurtfully, "You should have told Mom yourself. You always ran away crying, crybaby." I sometimes wonder if there weren't times he ran away crying too. Sometimes I think I was curious beyond my age. I mean, I know it might have been harmless child's play, except for how many times it happened. Actually, that doesn't really mean anything either, but I wonder if her age has to come into play. She wasn't anywhere near an adult. I really don't know why I didn't remember any of this until my late thirties and early forties. I don't even know why it is important now, except, like I said, it was the first time I remember being watched. It goes in line with my paranoia. It also goes in line with how I deal with everything. I override it and just go for long periods of time (months) without even giving it a second thought. I am able to do this successfully on and off for various reasons, but mostly medicines. The biggest reason I feel like it matters that I am being watched is when I have fallen off the bandwagon and gotten involved in substance abuse. It ties into the feeling of "I'm stupid" or "I wish I hadn't." The biggest thought of them all is "They know." It isn't until I have it out of my system that I don't worry about the repercussions of my actions. I am starting to crave being watched. It makes me feel alive, and that must be a double-edged disorder.

I have recalled many incidents, and I have several memories of her father catching this girl and me naked. I don't know how long he had been watching. The times he caught us were the most disturbing. I often wonder if they are the sole reason I was diagnosed as paranoid. It would seem logical to me. I also have to wonder if the girl who molested me was the victim of molestation herself. It is the only way the "little clues" fit in my mind. Thinking that helps me forgive her, and yet I almost always feel violated and dirty. Learning to forgive is a two-way street. You have to be mature enough to ask for forgiveness for your own faults before you fully understand the complexity of the act itself. It is a multifaceted thing that requires much thought. I think I am not being fair to her. I would like to think she was just experimenting. It definitely isn't fair to think she might have been molested when she might just have been sexually advanced for her age.

I did not realize that it was possible to bury something so deep that it was almost irretrievable. I locked the memories away for thirty-plus years. I had heard of people doing this, but I scoffed at it. When it happened to me, I was amazed, to say the least. I recall hearing someone say that molestation might be what makes a person gay. I seriously doubt it. The ways in which I woke to my sexuality were very much oriented to men. I had a female in my life I could have focused on, but I didn't. I remember my mother explaining the birds and the bees to me and it not making sense. I also remember her laughing (just a smirk, not at me) when I asked, "How will the man insert the penis when it's all squiggly?"

"You will know when the time is right," she said. Then she went into the kitchen and said something to my father about me not being old enough. Sometime after that, I was watching *Code Red*, and it started to work. I thought the firemen were hot. Maybe it's because I was a little pyromaniac before I burned myself, but that doesn't matter. I was in the living room and Mom said, "If you are going to do that, go to your room!" Evidently my body worked.

I don't want to make the girl out to be a villain. She wasn't a bad person. She was fun to play with and we did a lot of cool things. I liked her a lot. Anybody would have loved to have a cool older friend to play with, and that is what she was most of the time. It was when she didn't want my brother to play with us that bothered me. My brother would run home crying to Mom and calling me the crybaby. What is more baffling to me is how I can only remember the good times. Only now I can even remember a couple of times when I was curious enough to want to get undressed myself. I often wonder if those times were her fault at all, although she was older and should have put a stop to whatever happened. Well, sexual curiosity seems to have gotten the best of us.

Over the last couple of years, I have remembered many events, some of them in great detail. Most of them are completely innocuous. There was never any intent to injure. There were always times I felt caught or in the limelight. There was one time my brother tried to warn us that her father was coming, but it was too late. We couldn't get dressed in time. I remember her father looking down on us with contempt, and I knew she was in big trouble. But it didn't stop her from getting me naked. I knew that I would never be in trouble because my parents would never be told. In retrospect, I find this behavior very odd. My parents never knew anything until I told them in my early forties. They were shocked, to say the least.

The events happened many times, even in the bathroom of a church we did not attend. It was a church at the corner of one of the highways and a local street. We broke into the church bathroom and used it as our fort. It didn't seem to matter as long as it was semiprivate. There was one time in particular, in the church bathroom, where she had me on top of her in the missionary position. She was telling me what to do and all the time saying I wasn't doing it right. This is how I suspect she had been abused herself. It gives me chills to think how a thirteen-year-old could be telling a nine-year-old how to have sex properly. Regardless, I remember I left crying.

None of this makes any difference, except to mention the place where the schizoaffective paranoia started. I cannot begin to think that I would be completely normal if this hadn't happened. I just think it is where my disorders first reared their ugly heads. I might have imagined her father was watching because it was my hereditary or otherwise biological predisposition. I don't think so. It doesn't matter now that I have isolated it. It doesn't help to go over something and keep wishing things were different. Just move on and be free in the moment. It is said easier than done, I know. But it is what you have to do.

The mind has ways of protecting us from a lot of things. I often wonder how I am affected consciously if I am subconsciously repressing the memory of the events that took place forty years earlier. I also have a difficult time trying to sort out whether or not my experiences parallel those of other abused children. All sexuality seems weird to me; I have no basis for understanding "normal" sexuality. I used to think I had an advantage over people who weren't comfortable with homosexuals. I said, "If straights had to live the life of a fag for a second, they would pop." I assumed I understood why straights weren't comfortable. It took me many years to realize that we all are learning about each other. Who knows, I might be the one who'd pop if I were in somebody else's shoes. I started to open my eyes to how different people are and to see that people are not like me. I could not make the mistake of superimposing any of my beliefs onto anybody's fragile identity. Making this kind of mistake only divides us instead of bringing us closer. It is a social injustice that is woven into the very fiber of our being. The main question that remains for anybody is how long it takes one to see finally see the light. Most gay people understand that it isn't a choice—unless you are bisexual.

My grandmother never knew about my early life. I never had the recollections while she was alive. I find it very difficult to imagine what she would say. I vowed never to tell anyone about my burns or my sexuality. She used to let me dump all my problems onto her lap. When she felt that I needed to move on, she would say, "Other than that, you haven't got a thing to worry about." Sometimes it would make me mad, but most of the time I realized that I had been going on for too long. My grandmother had been married three times, and only the last husband did her right. That was by her admission. She had a hard go of it, and I am sure she would have some sage advice on how to deal with my situation. I often wonder if being a woman born in the 1920s with only one good arm had something to do with it. Did she have to settle for second-rate husbands? What were the circumstances of her marriages? She didn't talk about them, and every time I asked, I didn't get an answer. I wonder if my mother even knows.

My thought toward this matter makes me more appreciative of my caring family, and it definitely goes in line with my concept of finding my Vivid Blue. I learned that neither my reaction nor my response was my fault. Once again, I have found the search for a Vivid Blue in the lessons I have learned. Never would I have thought that my experiences would have been repressed, but since that was the case, I learned about myself in an immeasurable way. The search for a Vivid Blue takes me inward to the very center of my soul. It takes me to the place where the little child exists. The child who has never been hurt is the child I must hold onto for sanity's sake. Vivid

Blue is all about forgiveness. During times of great strife, I find that forgiveness is the greatest gift a human can give. I am learning to forgive myself for all my faults. I learned that forgiveness is a two-way street, and that in order to forgive in the manner that matters most, one must realize a need for forgiveness too. Maybe I need forgiveness for writing about all this.

Chapter 24. My Confused Thoughts

When I was younger, my grandmother and I used to play Scrabble. She would stand over my shoulder, look at the way I had my letters arranged, and then tell me I could do better. She loved the game and expected me to be a challenging opponent, even if she had to help me be that adversary. I learned to be a better player as a result. I told her she would always win if she knew the word I was playing. Just knowing the possible placement of my letters gave her an advantage. I told her that it wasn't fair, that it made me feel uncomfortable. None of this was enough to stop her from coaxing me to play my best. She never let me play subpar, and why should she? She paid me for playing my best game and scoring the highest number of points I could achieve. Therefore I would have to take back my letters until I got the maximum yield. Countless times she would tell me that I needed to shuffle the rack, or think about placing the words differently on the board. I was hesitant to put a new word down, even when it was the best option. I thought painstakingly about every move, but in doing so, I learned to think things through. There was real responsibility in mapping out the letters. When I won, which was rare, I had a great sense of accomplishment. I cannot believe I was paid for the education. I didn't just learn the simple things like words and strategies, or how to be a good sport. I learned how to keep on trying. I also learned something much more valuable, something only a loving relative could teach. My grandmother taught me that life is about perspective. Sometimes you have to rearrange your thoughts to get past your confusion.

I am willing to bet the majority of people who have a mental illness cannot come to grips with why they have been singled out for such a life-wrecking plight. I know if I think about it, it consumes me. I want to know everything about my disorders. Mostly I want to know about my schizoaffective disorder, because it is the thing I understand the least. I know the gist of it. Its most rudimentary definition is a psychotic person with significant depression or mania. The books and the Internet only go so far before they break schizoaffective disorder down into two groups, schizophrenia and a mood disorder. Schizoaffective disorder has two types, the depressed type and the bipolar type. I thought that since there are only two types of schizoaffective disorder, it should be easy to explain. I was wrong. All the books I bought said the exact same thing, but they left me feeling like I needed more information. I kept reading and thinking. I would have to dive into each separate subcategory. I chose to go with the only way I could comprehend it. My new concept would be "the sum of its parts equals the whole." Still, I couldn't get the word "schizophrenia" out of my mind. The mood disorder part was easier to understand, since I'd been diagnosed with bipolar some fifteen years prior.

According to the *Psychiatry Weekly* (5:21, August 30, 2010), which was speculating on the new *DSM-5* (Diagnostic and Statistical Manual of Mental Disorders), "when referring to the *DSM*'s write-up, there is evidence to suggest that schizoaffective disorder does not represent a distinct category from schizophrenia." I'm not even sure I read that correctly. I don't know why that still holds in my mind, but to me, it doesn't really matter if you say that I'm schizophrenic and have wild mood swings, or that I have wild mood swings and suffer from schizophrenic thoughts (psychosis). It is six of one, a half dozen of the other. Funny thing is, I look to recent books and articles and I get lost. I have to admit, I am not capable of thinking like a psychiatrist. I cannot take the knowledge and apply it to my life objectively. I know certain things about myself, but tying it all together doesn't work very well. I start to wonder how somebody with much more pronounced symptoms handles their situation. I wonder if our actions compare. At the same time, I really don't want to know.

I am reminded of an article I read on the Internet. There's one I can't find or document, so just bear with me. It said that police officers were asked to wear MP3 players while doing complex tasks like filling out resumes or playing cards. The MP3 players would scream out negative phrases. The police officers who endured this said that they worked through it (they did well), but they wondered how long it would take to wear them down. I can tell you it doesn't take very long for the average untrained person. That is what my paranoia is like, except I don't hear voices. I think repetitive thoughts. Mine are intense thoughts that never go away. At times they make me irrational. Thanks to my OCD, I cyclically think that I am going to be arrested or that I am being watched. I become convinced that somebody stole something or some of my medicine. I don't go for more than a few minutes before I have to tell myself there is no one out there. One of my biggest problems is thinking my house will be burglarized when I am gone. I cannot explain it on paper or in this book the way I live it in life. I have wondered at times if it is a form of hell on earth, except my logical mind has determined that there are many worse things. I choose not to compare it to others. It isn't fair to me, and it isn't fair to the ones with whom I am making the comparison. Some have it much worse, and of course, some manage it better. Whatever is, is. Relating this behavior to a clinical definition (or vice versa) requires stepping outside of one's own body. It isn't something very many people can do.

Just hearing the term "schizoaffective" rattles me. It is a whole lot of embarrassment wrapped up in a little ball. Immediately I have self-destructive thoughts. There is an overwhelming and uncontrollable urge to declare myself normal. After many years, I have learned not to overreact. I don't adopt my disorder willingly, and I assume many others in my situation don't either. I have no secret for managing my behavior, except for biting my tongue. It has never helped me to talk about it, not even to my therapist. I know that sounds weird. While my therapist is there to help and listen, talking about my schizoaffective disorder has left me with more questions. On the other hand, when it comes to my OCD or my PTSD, she has been quite helpful. I think it is because there is a bigger gray area as to why I am schizoaffective. I surely do feel the universe dealt me a bad card, but there is nobody to blame. I wouldn't take that copout even if I could.

I have grown accustomed to pretending my schizoaffective disorder doesn't exist. When I do think of it, the "schizo" part always bubbles to the top. I am a little obsessive about it. I am not okay with it. I think in terms of black and white. Is it wrong of me to think you're either full-blown ill or you're not? I know it doesn't work that way. In this case, you *can* be a little pregnant. You can have a moderate amount of delusion and still maintain some quite normal interactions with the real world. In my case, my paranoia led me to harmless yet weird behaviors. I did, however, go to great lengths to hide the disorders.

I have cycled in and out of delusions most of my life. I didn't realize it until the last cycle, when it got out of control. My schizoaffective disorder had many unexplainable components, and this time it was a beast for all to see. In the past, only a few really, really close friends knew I was paranoid. I was letting the "problem" spill over the top. Believing I was going to be arrested was one of the signature factors in my diagnosis. I also believed people were watching me and entering my home when I was out. The list of my disorders was getting longer. I had no valid reasons why this was happening. Everybody who knew me knew this was a problem, but they didn't know what to do about it. I began to think all of my friends knew. I was going to the psychiatrist, and I was taking my medicine. The medicine wasn't working. My closest friends did their best to reassure me that I was in error with my paranoid thoughts. They also did their best to reassure me that people were not doing what I was accusing them of doing. Of course, I wasn't blaming anybody specifically. I was using my signature phrases like "they will" and "they are." My parents did notice but had no idea what to do. I remember Dad confronting me and demanding to know, "Who is 'they'?" but I had no answer. My biggest fear was "they are breaking into my house." Still I could not answer who "they" were.

"Confused thoughts" is the nice way of saying you're delusional. It wasn't registering at the time. As a matter of fact, it took quite some time for me to come to that realization. It took even longer to come to the even more important conclusion that I wasn't crazy. I was taking antipsychotic medications, but that didn't prove anything conclusively. I needed to brush up on my deductive reasoning skills before I made myself look bad. I also needed to give myself a break. I couldn't say, "Hey, everything is going to be all right," because I wasn't sure. Next I had to really find out about schizoaffective disorder. The short little definition they'd given me in the hospital wasn't going to get me very far. The Internet didn't go very far either, and neither did all the books I'd bought.

Schizoaffective disorder had the same standard definition throughout. I was very disappointed.

I needed know how "confused" I was. It really isn't something you can quantify, but I set my feeble mind to finding out. I wasn't going to sit by and idly accept it. Well, I take that back. After a while I had to accept it, because I knew I was running up against a brick wall. I realized the most basic thing about confusion in general: you can be a little confused or a lot confused. You can switch back and forth at any given time. It is kind of like using a road map. You have to start somewhere. That is a very hard thing to do when you just start looking at the lines all over a sheet of paper. Once you get your bearings, you might have the right state but not know the right city. That is really, really, really confusing. If you are finally in the right state and city on the map but looking in the wrong section of town, that is really, really confusing. If you are in the right city, right section of town, and on the right street but can't find the house, that is just confusing. It is all a matter of degree. Of course, there is the argument that you don't know what you are looking for, and in that case you really would be crazy. In any case, I knew I needed to ask for help. I needed help in both understanding what schizoaffective meant as well as understanding what my symptoms were.

Dealing with the schizoaffective diagnosis was hard. I got the news by myself, and I dealt with it myself. This lasted for at least a very lonely week or so. Then I told my mother. She was caught a little off guard and asked why I had waited so long to tell her. I didn't think it was something you just blurted out. Then I told my friend John. I waited a month or so to tell my father, because I didn't know how he would take it. He said "everybody" was mentally ill, but to what degree? Wow, I didn't understand that. I have never formally told my brother. I know he knows about my paranoia, and he has reasons to suspect my bouts of delusions. We don't discuss it, except for him to tell me to stay away from drugs. He has caught me doing drugs in the distant past and thinks I act very strange when I am high. I probably do. Anyway, I am wandering far from the topic. It is the nature of the disorder.

I started to become obsessed with the definition of

schizoaffective a few short months after getting out of the hospital. That would be fall of 2011. I started to look up the definition and found it to be lacking in every source. Then I went to the library and couldn't get anything, even through interlibrary loan. I bought every book I found on Amazon and realized that each one only repeated verbatim what the others said. I could go through the motions here, but I won't waste your time, and it won't help me or you understand. I turned to the *DSM*, and it broke the disorder down in ways I wasn't prepared to go. No, I was looking at my disorder by my symptoms. I wanted to know, Why me? What can be done? What are the causes? These questions are all unanswerable. Now, in my opinion, my college education was useless. Well, that isn't fair to me or my fellow graduates. My degree would only help in ways not quantifiable in this application. I had all the books and had copied passages from the *DSM*, and I still needed more information. The *DSM* was telling me to look under two different categories, bipolar and schizophrenic. Now I was back to the "confused thoughts" question. I knew I was schizophrenic. According to one definition, I only had a "low-calorie" version. This version was where I was just a little less "schizo" and a lot more affective. I hope that is the case, but I truly act paranoid. Yes, I acted very paranoid. Maybe it depends on the person. I was confused and have remained confused to this day. I know it isn't because I am lacking in intelligence. It is because they don't have it ironed out and I don't fit any mold.

It was all downhill from there. Even now, I am still at a loss for a complete definition of schizoaffective disorder. I can regurgitate the books and the *DSM-5*. It really does boil down to my symptoms. I look at my disorder and what I do that interrupts my life. It is a strange way to look at my life. It is better for me to realize that I can work with my actions, behaviors, and attitudes. I have no control of my disorders. I will leave all the analyzing up to the experts. Their research is priceless for all of us, but I cannot be objective when I am suffering from my delusions. I am not sure any schizoaffective person can; it is the nature of the disorder. I will try to control what I can.

I hope people understand. I feel confident that I can tell most of my friends. At the same time, I realize there is little point in opening the door to rejection and discrimination. I hope that people can be intelligent and caring and ultimately want others to make it through their adversity. They might even realize some have harder lives than others. Life doesn't play fair, but sometimes things work out. I know I could write some spiteful words here, but the people those words were intended to reach won't be reading my book. They aren't the type to see themselves in my words, either. The ones who have been kind, caring, and generous members of society will already know without my having to tell them. The least judgmental are the ones who quietly gloss over somebody's failures and patiently wait for another time for them to get it right. It is what Vivid Blue is all about.

Chapter 25. Some Sample Writing

A day in the life of someone else is probably twenty-three-and-a-half hours too many. I took the time to pick out a sample of my thought processes to give you a better idea of what I go through on a daily basis. If you see any imperfection in my writing, it is my goal, and please forgive me. I do this to illuminate that my disorder is not due to a violent tendency or even self-destructiveness (anymore). I think it took a vast amount of courage to place this chapter here. I also think I have gotten over my problem, because I don't care. It is just stuff, and the really important things in life are the people who love me, and my loving pets. So take a gander at what a paranoid person thinks about before medication and therapy do their magic. Then again, this might be psychobabble.

***

I stumbled and fumbled around my house, trying to make head or tails out of my life. I have to convince myself that my very existence gives me the right to have my point of view. I don't have it all figured out. The world in which I live is ever changing, and I have to morph with it. I bend and shape my life to the constant twisting of circumstances and events. I get pulled in directions my imagination can never foresee. Along with this twisted thought process, my outlook changes. The resiliency expected by friends, family, and heck, even society is daunting. It is crucial to keep a positive outlook, for me and for them.

I have to ponder why I feel a need to emphatically state my right to my point of view. I believe it comes from my insecurities. I cannot presume to think everybody has these insecurities or a need to justify their point of view. I am quite sure there are people who don't even give it a second thought. Funny, I don't wish I were one of those people. I can only speak for myself, and I have a hard time doing that. For me, being schizoaffective means misjudging certain things. I try to think I am not paranoid, but it doesn't work that way.

I almost always have to forgive myself for thinking bad thoughts about other people. I have to think that people wouldn't be as cruel as I project them to be. Yes, project. It is a long story, but to be paranoid or diagnosed with paranoia, you have to believe people are doing things to you. I have proof of the things that make me paranoid. Unfortunately, nobody else has seen or believed the things that have been happening to me. It elicits the standard "I believe you *think* this is happening" crap.

There, I said it. So "I must be on that kick again," as my father puts it. Sure, I say. Proof is in a suspicious e-mail and many other things I choose not to get into. The e-mail sender has all the makings of a serial stalker. Yet I deduced it was just somebody messing with me. The other things add up, but not to anybody else. They are just the sort of thing somebody would do to mess with a paranoid person. Why? It is anybody's guess. If I were to make a conjecture, it would surely sound implausible and create quite the stir. It doesn't really matter. I'm not going to play into it. It is my belief, and I know nobody else will believe me. So I must endure the abuse and know that it will never get any worse or that they will tip their hand. It is one of those "we can play this all day." As a matter of fact, I can say I'm winning. They are jumping through hoops to try to rattle me, and it isn't working. They have entered my house and I don't care. I have purposely left everything the way it is just to invite them back. They steal my Xanax a few pills at a time and hope I won't notice, but I counted them just yesterday. I told everybody somebody will try to use them against me someday. I have quit pestering my friends and family because I know they don't deserve to be bothered. Whatever "they" might do will be a shock, but it won't be enough to get me to crumble. I am learning acceptance. Now that I know it is them and not me, I know there is no action that requires my attention. I am free in a sense. They have used little tricks on my computer and cell phone, and my father will be the first to say that's impossible. It's not, and we (I am projecting) all know it. I have built a new attitude of forgiveness for the ones who are sick, and most often I come to the conclusion that I am a better person than somebody who would mess with somebody's head. It helps me to know I am a forgiver. It is sad to think there are people out there who would relinquish their dignity so quickly. It is sad to know there are people not capable of forgiving.

I could list page after page of the things that have happened. I realize now that it started over ten years ago. I almost went bananas four or five years ago. I consider that the time when they almost got me. They were so close, but whoa. Now I know, and I never plan to care that much again. I will have to take the loss of everything I hold dear as a start, because that is what they want. I am prepared mentally. If I have my friends, family, and felines, I will be okay. I love life. I am not going to give in to paranoid thoughts. I have learned to say that every paranoid thought is an opportunity to tell myself it is going to be a good day. I have so much to be thankful for, probably more than the people who are trying to pull me down. Heck, they wouldn't be trying to pull me down if they had a life of their own outside of mine. There I go again; I'm falling prey to thinking about them. I have better things to do, like putting myself in check.

I like knowing I put myself in check. It gives me a sense of security knowing I'm right with my maker, and knowing I wouldn't treat a person in certain ways. I don't want to be the kind of person who walks through this world and inflicts pain and suffering on somebody else. I want to be a caring and compassionate soul capable of forgiving. I like knowing I follow the golden rule. I have always hoped people would see me as gentle and compassionate. I don't ever act on these paranoid thoughts. While they sometimes enter my mind, they never control my actions. I tell myself, "It is never okay to make somebody feel bad." And as my friend John puts it, "What can you do about it right now?" It's always nothing.

What then do we do when confronted with a major flaw? I am referring to the ones I have made just as much as the ones that have been perpetrated against me, or against anybody else, for that matter. There is not a soul that has walked this earth that hasn't made mistakes when dealing with another fellow human. The key then becomes a matter of forgiveness. Forgiveness is a two-way street. Oh, standing and preaching is what I never intended to do. So why did I even choose to write this lopsided little story? It is not that I need to be reminded of anything, that's for sure. It is always the people who have a conscience who suffer the most. I am horribly regretful of my past, that is for sure. There is a little saying: "The person I am hates the person I used to be."

***

Back to the question of why I chose to put this here. First let me say, I don't know when I wrote it. I wish I could use just one line, something like "simply put" or "frankly speaking," but I can't. The reason I chose to write this is because my karma stinks. I've offended the gods that be. Yes, my attitude stinks too. I have a whole history of life events that have led me here, and the road has been long. I am not going to make this little tidbit a "don't do this" story. I am going to turn it all around and pull from a conversation I had with my mother. She asked me a question about my youth. I didn't give her the response she was looking for.

She asked me whether or not I had a problem with school at a very young age. She assumed I did. I told her I didn't. She rephrased the question, thinking she could trick it out of me, but I still responded that all was typical until sixth grade. She wanted me to say I had a problem beginning in second grade, because that was when a major life change happened: she moved us from regular school to private school. She thought it was a lot for me. Never once did I think I would blow my mother out of the water when I broke the news that halfway through sixth grade was more than a little tough. Actually, I said it a little more strongly, regrettably so. It only added to my mother's fixation. It is a problem with me. I can't seem to say the right things. Some people fixate on the words and can't forgive my accidental statements.

I want to blame this on two immediate members of my family. But at some point you have to adopt your problems as your own. I lip off with a callous manner, and it is sour to say the least. When I am not being flippant with my comments, I am too silent, and the assumptions fly from my overloaded lips. Oh, what I have done to wreck my integrity. Years cannot repair what a youthful stupidity has damaged. I can only try to dig myself out of this hole by watching what I say, and I have never tried that before.

This is the point where my thoughts always seem to wander. I have projected that people aren't willing to forgive because I haven't forgiven myself. It is unfair to assume that people lack the ability to be the caring and understanding individuals God created. It is a major flaw with me, and one that I must work on every day. I will rise above my petty feelings. I don't have to think I am being singled out as unforgiving..

If you believe in forgiveness, then forgiveness exists. There is some comfort in knowing that people think what they want to believe, but then again, that turns it all around back to me. I have to work on me. Wow. What a chore this can be. That is a whole lot of vivid in my search.

Chapter 26. I Just Do

All self-help books start to sound the same. So what makes mine any different? I could start off with a bunch of pithy-sounding crap, but I hope won't bore you. It isn't my intent to offend you. I want my book to be a casual conversation about my life and about how I keep moving forward. You are probably asking, "How *do* you keep moving forward?" The answer might surprise you. I just do. Yes, that is right. You read me correctly. Close the book or move to the next chapter, because that is my answer. I just do. I hope people can relate. There are no secrets for me other than trying. I just do. I love saying that. There is satisfaction in boiling it down to a simple little sentence I can rely on when times get tough. When asked, I get to have a long conversation that is briefly summed up by "I just do." It is so ironic that I have to giggle. Like you, I sometimes wish I could convince myself it were that easy. I really do. Why did I choose to write something like that in a book, you ask? Well, I feel like a SABP survivor should be the one to write a book. Yes, I do feel that the schizoaffective people in this world have merit just moving forward. Others might disagree. Either way, I chose to write it because I wanted you to understand what being schizoaffective is all about.

First and foremost, being schizoaffective is not saying I am totally or merely schizophrenic. I am not differentiating myself, because that is merely nitpicking. Still, it took a long time to convince me that schizoaffective wasn't just schizophrenic plus another ailment, or in my case, two ailments. Actually, I still may be wrong, and depending on the doctor, you get a different answer. Just using the "schizo" part fooled me too. It was when I looked up what it meant that I started to understand. I hate the complete term they use for me, which is "schizoaffective bipolar type." You know by now, it basically means I have confused thoughts and bipolar actions. My paranoia is extreme. Other people are a little more fortunate. My medicine cabinet is full of mood stabilizers, antidepressants, and antipsychotic drugs. In fact, the antipsychotic medicine I am taking right now is a high dose. We will probably have to change my whole routine if we change now. I will get back to my case in a little bit.

The best source of knowledge pertaining to schizoaffective disorder can be found in what is called the *DSM-5*, which stands for *Diagnostic and Statistical Manual of Mental Disorders*, fifth edition. The book is designed to help psychiatrists and psychologists accurately diagnose patients. The first edition came out in 1952, and the current version was published in 2014. In addition, there are a couple of books that I couldn't get through interlibrary loan, so I bought them for myself. Other than that, there isn't much written on my condition. Just thinking I would be categorized into a group of people they really don't know much about is frightening.

Trying to self-diagnose is pointless. I will say that I know my schizophrenic tendencies are more problematic than most. Here comes another tricky part: I am, by every definition, bipolar. The vast numbers of books on the subject of bipolar disorder do apply to me. So why can't I call myself both schizophrenic and bipolar? Because the way I interpret it, schizoaffective has its own category, and it is a far trickier diagnosis than either disorder by itself. I am not at all saying it is worse, just trickier. There are many in the psychiatric field who believe it is indistinguishable from its subcomponents, however. This includes those who published the new *DSM-5*. The main problem (in my opinion) is they still don't have enough information to go on. I hope I didn't confuse you. It is, after all, a very complex subject. It is well over my head.

I know my past drug usage made it difficult for doctors to determine whether or not I was schizoaffective. It is an underlying factor. I think the results of any drug-related behavior manifest themselves in unwanted symptoms, but maybe this is the most recurring and residual of all. I will always regret the days of my youth when I trashed my body. I wish I believed that my drug usage was the cause for the whole thing, but I honestly believe it was the other way around. My schizophrenic behavior led to my drug usage. Many a great mind has thought it to be a chicken-or-egg scenario. Who knows? There are statistics to prove that drug usage is extremely high in schizoaffective people. I am very weak when it comes to temptation and I work very hard at being clean. It seems to me there is a correlation between my stress and probability.

Now that I have sufficiently side tracked you, we will get back to discussing my schizoaffective behavior. When I ask for more information on schizoaffective disorders, I always get referred back to the *DSM*. I must always try to look at my actions objectively and see if I fit the classification. It doesn't help that my actions match several classifications individually and then one as a whole. In my opinion, the doctors are really making an educated guess. There are many reasons for the guess. Well, well, now, "guess" isn't fair is it? It is a call, though, by every stretch of the imagination. I used to think maybe I fit all three diagnoses—just plain paranoid, bipolar, and schizophrenic—but I have come a long way. Explaining that I have parts of all three but not all three in their entirety is more difficult than I realized. Whew!

Delusional paranoia is a key component of schizoaffective disorder, as Martine Daniel explains in her book *Schizoaffective Disorder Simplified*: "Delusions that center on a person being watched or being persecuted are known as paranoid delusions" (p. 53). This is one of my biggest problems. Well, that, and worry. In any case, I have always felt that somebody from the big entities (police, FBI, CIA, etc.) has been watching me. When my meds are working like they should, I realize it is just a feeling I get, and I need to override the emotions. Part of what Daniel writes is that the subject will irrationally use anything he or she can to back up these feelings. I did this too. I would assume that any click on the phone meant there was a wiretap. It wasn't until I got the right kind of medication at the proper dosage that I believed there were nothing but bad emotions and feelings dominating my every move. It was then that I didn't care.

From both Martine Daniel's book and the Internet, I have gathered that one in two hundred people have or are suffering from schizoaffective disorder. That number seems a little high to me, but I am quoting from her introduction, where she goes on to say that is 0.5 percent of the population. Another little tidbit I learned is that women are more likely to be schizoaffective than men. I do know several people from my group meetings who suffer from the same plight. It's weird, though—we all happen to be male.

So why am I telling you all this? Because I believe most of the sixty-million-plus diagnosed mentally ill patients can be fully functional in society. Sure, there are a large number who are beyond help. There are still those who need just a little help to be completely normal in a complex world. Let's face it, we all have to make adjustments to survive in this world. I am smart enough to know that even the sane ones have problems too. I ran in denial of my problems for years until I finally faced them. Funny thing about denial is that you can go back and forth with it for years. I did. I believed for a year or two that I was bipolar. That was just in the beginning. Then I believed I wasn't bipolar. Then I believed I was again, and I would be cured after a while (little did I know). After it was all said and done, I started to write a book to convince myself that it was actually happening to me. I needed convincing that my life was a wreck. Well, my life was wrecked. How did that happen? How did it happen to me? Well, it did. Going to the gym wasn't going to fix it either, so I quit. Taking medicines would only make the train go in one direction. How was I going to get on track? I still don't have the answer, and I am approaching fifty. How is my book going to help you when I am not sure I can help myself? Well, maybe we're in this boat together.

Once again I have wandered far from the topic at hand. I was in the middle of explaining my situation and I got sidetracked. Most of my problems are self-generated. By that I mean problems created by my magnificent little mind. Without going into details, I will basically state that if my mind could downshift and see all the little things that were going on, I would be better off. I race from one conclusion to the next without stopping. I am so quick to make up my mind that things are a certain way. I have on many a day locked myself in my bedroom after convincing myself it was a rainy day, only to come out and find the sun fully shining. My mind plays tricks on me. It isn't fair what I do to myself. I tell myself, "One day I'll learn," but I never do. It is my mind that controls every aspect of my disorder. Without medication, my mind wanders in directions I find impossible to control.

Speaking of medicine, every time I take mine, I wish I didn't

161

have to take it. But the truth is, I will always have to take it. I will take it or some form of it for the rest of my life. I know it. When I take the meds, they make me feel bad. It isn't the mental realization that hurts; it isn't just the way the meds make me feel physically. I do get a yucky feeling when I take them. I take them at night to get the feeling over with, and then I can start the next day without the physical feelings. Basically, I sleep through the yucky times. What really bothers me is the thought of being tied to them. The thought that wacky is just two missed doses away. It is also the thought that I am tied to a pharmacy and cannot go on a month-long camping trip.

My delusional side is controlled by antipsychotic drugs. There are several to choose from, and who knows what will be next, or what will happen when I switch to the new ones? The worst thing would be to have another episode(s). My delusion consists of not trusting people and their motives. Actually, trust issues run amok. I also suspect the motive for people doing things, especially things that happen in my absence. I realize that the world moves without my control and there is nothing I can do about it. That bothers me. For example, I worry about my cats and how they are doing in my absence. I cannot control their actions, but I would if I could. It is a comfort to know I don't have to worry about their motives. In fact, I worry about everything that goes on in my house in my absence.

My bipolar swings are controlled by antidepressants and mood stabilizers. For this I take several medications in combination. This is another area where my situation gets even trickier. I am considered a rapid cycler, which means I shift quickly from manic to depressed states. I think it takes triggers, but my psychiatrist (not to put words in anybody's mouth) tells me that I don't need a trigger to cycle. This part of my schizoaffective disorder was the easiest to diagnose. It wasn't until they matched up the paranoid thoughts with the bipolar actions that they realized I was schizoaffective. I often wonder if this changed or if it was always this way. Either way, it is that way now, and it has been diagnosed.

There are many times I have alluded to being embarrassed by my situation. Who wouldn't be a little embarrassed? It goes with the territory. To claim I'm not would be a bald-faced lie. There are times I want to hide my book and never let a soul see it. Then I come to grips with everything and decide that it is better to let people read about my struggles in the hope that it helps somebody else. Helping, for some, is human nature, and through others we see ourselves. I am not saying everybody who reads this will see a part of himself, but maybe he will understand a little bit more.

The easiest thing to do is bury your head in the sand and pretend that life works itself out. I'm a realist. Sometimes that is the key to survival, sometimes it isn't. Sometimes you have to look at your cards and make choices based on what you think is right for you. There is never a bad time to learn something new about yourself. I take comfort in having a little knowledge about myself. There really isn't such a thing as a blind decision if you know a little about the creature you're dealing with. I can't say it wasn't a little luck that brought me to this point, but I can say I paid attention to some of the clues that were presented to me. With a little help from the friends who have faith in me, I will go far. It is through their eyes that I see myself and can move forward. My search for a Vivid Blue is about recognizing the things that will propel me into the next wave, especially the positive ones.

Chapter 27. Staying Positive in What Can Be a Negative World

If you let it, life can be overwhelming. Some days I get so preoccupied that I don't even notice time slipping away. These are the good days. Then there are the other days when there is nothing but the slow, methodical tick of the clock crawling by at an agonizing pace. It is during these torturous seconds that I find myself in need of a positive attitude. For some reason, when I am busy, I manage to be happier than when I am idle. I am programmed that way. Staying busy is difficult, primarily because I'm lazy. I guess that is my problem. Periodically I have too much time to think. I think with a great amount of mental error too. By now I have to acknowledge my disorders. They have been with me long enough. It seems pointless to wish my life were better. I, like many, have remained in denial to my detriment. This so-called self-realization isn't supposed to be a put-down. I need to address my situation. I have been to many doctors and counselors over the years, and they all say the same thing: I have a chronic mental illness, and thus I cannot separate myself from millions of Americans. I don't like being reminded that I fit in this category. It doesn't help to think that it is not a discriminatory disease. It can strike at any age, and it is anyone's guess who will fall prey to the ailment. I want answers. Why can't I have normal life like the rest of society? Pretty soon I am comparing myself others and saying things like "At least I don't have it as bad as so-and-so." I try to run from terms that I hate and the terms that seem to hurt, like "dysfunctional." There is no way to tidy up the mess I created in the past. It leaves little doubt in my mind as to why mentally ill people can get wrapped up in negative thinking.

I am not a motivational speaker, nor would I want to be. I think motivational speakers have to be one of a kind. Encouraging an audience to move forward and bringing life to a crowd takes a gift that few people possess. I do, however, envy their ability to stay positive. They seem to have an infinite supply of energy and the uncanny ability to say the right things. A lot can be learned from them. I have often wondered what their low moments were like. Do they feel the same lows as the average person? Can they relate to a person who suffers from depression? Are these motivational speakers exempt from the world in which people with schizoaffective disorders live? A normal person might think that is a dumb question. An emotionally charged SABP person would argue till he was blue in the face. Anyway, these questions will never be answered to my satisfaction, but if you ask me, people like that probably do feel sufficient lows. They probably have excellent ways to cope too. They definitely have a system of turning depression around into something positive. This system probably makes it seem like everything is going right. You never hear them talk about their depression in the same way as a mentally ill person lives his life. I imagine they could use any one of us as a reason or cause to move forward and not fall back in some fashion. They are always talking about their keys to success. They talk about the future like it will magically turn into something spectacular, a gold-plated dream, if you will. They certainly allude to a financial past that made them want to get up on a stage and tell us exactly how to live our lives. They say this past of theirs was enough to make them change. I don't want to make callous statements, but their past can't compare to our present nightmare. They probably haven't spent any time in the hospital trying to get their life back together following a psychotic meltdown. But I digress. Anyway, they obviously put their depression aside long enough to convince a large group of people that they don't suffer from the devastating plight. The thing we need to do is learn from them and not become bogged down with the feeling that we will never be able to achieve what they are promoting.

Going to a seminar is supposed to be a positive, uplifting experience. It is designed that way, and for the goal-oriented individual, it works wonders. I went to a few seminars when I worked out at the local research park. I never saw the greats like Zig Ziegler, but all the speakers still by definition gave a motivational speech. They made me feel like I could follow their advice and change my world. It was always about change. Change is the core concept of the motivational speech. At least that has always been my interpretation. You're supposed to exchange the bad habits for good habits, the bad thought processes for positive ones. When I got there, I thought, "I can do this." This was all before my disorders started rearing their ugly heads, or at least before we noticed them, and before I got stabilized on my medications. Relating my disorders to motivational speeches has gotten me to thinking: How are people with disorders supposed to gather what we need for our personal development? Going to these seminars doesn't seem to fit us as a group. We aren't really their target audience, are we? Most mentally ill people don't get up and do an eight-to-five job religiously. We have, regardless of how hard the speaker tries to convince us otherwise, a different set of circumstances. We might wake to the same depressing factors that their audience does, like bad finances. We also have car troubles, domestic issues, and quite often families who need us. We know what it is like to have to put a roof over our heads. The main difference is we have to pay expensive medical bills and for medications. The caveat is we most likely have poor job rates and a few work-related skeletons in our closets. The difference here is a major illness. It is one that can't be easily explained away. We have more problems holding us back and fewer opportunities for advancement. I say it is all the more reason to have a better outlook on life.

Regardless of the fact that we don't fit into that seminar group, we can emulate the motivational speaker. It always helps to pattern your life after somebody who has made it. For some, reading the books of the great motivational speakers is a start, but I tend to stick to the books by the less famous. I want to know how someone similar to me, suffering from schizoaffective disorder, OCD, and PTSD, handles a day they manage to make work, despite their adversity. It doesn't help me to know that there is such a big gap between myself and somebody who makes a million dollars. I don't want to compare myself to a millionaire. Sure, I strive for a million, but realistically I'm not there. I have my own way of rationalizing the fact that I don't make a million. I tell myself a million would ruin my life. I almost always think millionaires never truly think about the less fortunate. I tell myself if they did, they wouldn't be opposed to taxes that help out our communities and our roads. I would love to pay the taxes on a million, because I would be making a million. Of course, my rationalizations aren't fair to the people who do make a million. I end up taking a long route of thoughts, only to come back to a point where I think I have been lucky. I have to literally think about being lucky. When I am lucky enough to have clients, I make a lot more than minimum wage. When I wasn't making anything, my family was there to help me out. It turns out I have always been lucky and blessed to have a lot of good things. Usually I come to the conclusion that I am being very narrow-minded. In the past I looked at that little sliver of somebody else's life and told myself that my life was bad. How could I stop this bad thought process from happening again? It seems to be a recurring fault of mine. I don't think it was something my parents taught me. They did their level-headed best to keep me positive and moving forward. It was very easy to see what I wanted in somebody else's life. Of course, other people only display what they want me to see. They are not advertising the bad, and who can blame them?

I remember in great detail the monumental failures that keep me from feeling normal. It isn't enough that I keep a mental diary of them, I have to add negative thoughts so I make sure I don't forget. It is a pattern I have noticed, and it spells disaster for my already weak self-esteem. I live the thoughts of "the boy who blew himself up." I have to work very hard to hold my head up. I know I have to make a conscientious effort to eliminate the bad thought process from dominating. If I could just remember that I am human and therefore entitled to make mistakes, I would have the world as my oyster. Why I can't remember it is the real question. That is ironic, the fundamental error. It's the same with the motivational speeches. While you are in the audience, you think, "I can do this." When you get home, it's a whole different story. Why does this happen time and again? I know why, it is my disorders. It isn't just a choice like the ever-so-optimistic people would have me believe. It is so easy to wake up and start the day negatively! I have answers that could fill a boat for why the world is falling apart. Trying to find reasons for the beautiful day it is outside is real work, especially when my body screams something different. When I think about it, I can logically deduce that life is all about choices. My logic tells me I choose to wallow in my misery. My logic also tells me to look at the things that are right in my life. I can find slivers of both good and bad, and logic tells me they are almost equally proportioned. I just can't manage to stop the bad feelings, even though I am saying, "Cheer up." I logically recognize that my chemical balance is messed up. I think it is important to stay positive when your body is giving you these wrong signals.

I'm sure only bad things come from negative thoughts. I'm told over and over again that it is called a self-fulfilling prophecy, and I'm willing to bet schizoaffective people are among the best at making them. If you act on a bad feeling, you will make a bad choice. If you make a bad choice once, chances are you will the next time too. It will just compound itself, and then you really will feel bad. Something deep inside tells me it doesn't have to be this way. I love it when I reverse the negative process. It isn't as simple as doing something positive. One positive act in a sea of negative action will go unnoticed. It is there. It's like seeing the carpet through all the cat hair—it's there. The question becomes how we clean up the mess. First and foremost we must believe we can do something to make it better. This is the main reason I stay on my medication. I don't preach it, it just happens to be the smart thing for anybody looking to be positive. Absolute negative action is not taking your meds, or not seeking medical help.

Your outlook in life says a lot about you. It predicates how you deal with others. A mentally ill person's outlook is tainted, and his relationship with others is strained. I was once given this little snippet on Facebook. It went something like this: "A dog entered a room of mirrors and came out snarling and growling. Then another dog entered the same room of mirrors and came out happy and cheerful. It was all how they looked at life." I agree, and I try to live by those words of wisdom. I still can't help that my disorder takes over. I admit I suffer from a touch of schizophrenia, and I have confused thoughts. I distrust strangers as a general rule. I can try to rationalize it by saying I have been through a lot, and it is true, I have. I think that my past has more to do with my future, and I get caught in a loop. It won't do any good to try to explain it, because I have been trying to explain it for years. I will just say there are many reasons I cannot override what is inside my head. Then the real work comes in. It is a matter of self-preservation. In reality, I happen to be lucky. I can still use logic to override my disorder. I can still think my way past the feelings that dominate me. The same logic that allows me to override the confused thoughts allows me to keep positive in this ever-so-negative world of mine. For me, logic gets stronger the more I use it. It is like witchcraft. I realize there are many less fortunate who have a harder struggle. I realize their extreme cases of mental illness dictate their feelings and actions. I have a great deal of sympathy for them. How they deal day to day is beyond me. They deserve more credit than society gives them. Staying positive for them might not be a choice. Then again, maybe staying positive is the only way they make it.

There you go. I am not a motivational speaker, but this was my most motivational chapter. Think of yourself as a mini motivational speaker and give yourself pep talks. If you try, you can learn to stay positive in this negative world. There are always things that will trip you up, but conscious effort and planning can save you from the pitfalls. Cherish your pets if you have them; above all, look for reasons to be there for your little buddies. Remember not to push people away, and always, always try to rule out the external factors that will drag you down. If you cannot separate the problems, then you cannot solve the problems.

Chapter 28. What to Do with a Day

Some days it can be the hardest thing in the world to get out of bed. There is, after all, nobody to give me a pep talk, and nobody to remind me that my life isn't always as bad as it seems. Depression is king, and the only way to avoid suffering is to ignore my life completely. When I finally do get out of bed, I move very slowly. If I move, I have a routine, and it always helps to get into it as fast as I can. The sooner I get going, the sooner I get past my problems. I have a lot of reasons to get my day started, but quite often I don't see them until I look.

Just after the dichotomy of my decision to get out of bed, the shower beckons me. That is, unless I start to write. I like to write; it soothes my soul. My next statement isn't an original thought, and I probably should be crediting somebody somewhere, but here goes: "Writing is like babbling on paper, except you get to come back and change your mistakes." So if I am lucky, the inspiration will hit, and I will slap something on paper. Writing often dictates a slack morning routine, with a shower later in the day. Sometimes the shower won't be until right before I go out for dinner. It's sad to say, but I have nobody to answer to but my cats. When I write, I can either be positive or negative, and it plays out in the tone of my words. Quite often I have to rewrite the negative parts, because it's inappropriate to complain on paper when I have so much control over what I put down with my pen. I don't want my book to be a sob story, yet I do want my audience to relate to a life that has been, to say the very least, challenging. After all, I am writing a book about being schizoaffective.

I will consciously choose to write or to take a shower at the beginning of the day. It is how I will handle my life, or at least the day in front of me. It works for me. I admit, on the mornings I take a shower, I function better. Or should I say I am at least able to function right out of bed. I have exceptions to all of this, and that is what being schizoaffective is about.

As a general rule, life isn't rosy when you take little pills to make you feel better. Chances are you wouldn't be reading my book if you wanted to read a little fantasy. So I look to find slices of heaven where I can, and I try to completely drown out the thoughts that aren't helpful to my well-being. For inspiration, I look to my two cats. One is named Sebastian (nicknamed Sea Bass) and the other Sophie. Sea Bass is a tuxedo Norwegian forest cat, and Sophie is pure white. Together they make the most elegant couple you could ever imagine. But Sophie has a flaw: she has to be the center of attention, and I don't say that lightly. When I write, she is right there with me. She sometimes lies in the center of my back, dead on top of me, as I stretch across my bed. She has to lie on me when I watch TV, and what's more, she has to be on my feet as I sleep. I have created a monster. All this aside, she is my comfort and my inspiration, especially when I am just journaling or writing for my book. She will lie there for hours if I let her, and she always grumbles if I make her move. I do my best work when she is near. She is my caregiver, and she never lets me feel down. For his part, Sea Bass brings me up and shows me how to be happy and carefree. They are a schizoaffective person's dream team. My morning is complete with them.

My cats help me keep a positive mental attitude, but it isn't as easy as looking down or just petting them. I still have to work very hard on my mental maturity, and it didn't come overnight, either. During my time in the hospital, I realized that other people couldn't help me with my problems. As a matter of fact, other people were a direct cause of my problems. Well, I should say that the way I felt they looked at me was the cause of my problems. I'm not talking about my paranoia. I assumed people saw me like I saw myself, chipped and damaged. You know, they saw me with my disorder. One of the things I realized in the hospital was I didn't need to worry about others' opinions. I might have realized it, but I still can't quite get there. It is hard to do with a mental disorder. Heck, just say the last sentence out loud and tell me if you don't think the last two words win as the subject of the sentence. My negativity toward my life and my circumstance was a preconditioned factor. I woke feeling that way, both chemically and mentally. It never changed. I was the expert at hiding it. Okay, I wasn't even an expert at hiding it, and the people who knew didn't know what to do.

It is easier to stay positive if you rule out external factors that might be pulling you down. For some it might just be a rainy day. I happen to love rainy days, because I can write. I may be different, but I do have plenty of other things pulling me down. For anyone else, maybe there is tension with a close family member, maybe even with a family member who has passed away. Maybe you have a toothache or a leg pain. You might have been harboring bad feelings toward a boss or a parent. Each of these is a stressor and can cause you to be negative. It only takes one stressor, but if you have a combination, watch out. The best way to deal with them is to recognize them for what they are, and then make a conscious effort to not let them ruin your attitude. Remember, staying positive is our goal. Another thing: people will tell you to "just get over it" or "just be happy." They don't know what you're going through. They can't possibly know unless they are schizoaffective too. Be careful with this philosophy, though, because the reverse is also true: you can't possibly know what it's like to be them, either. I have a chapter on making yourself happy, but I don't just say unsympathetically, "Deal with it."

Whatever you do, don't push away the people who love you. This only hurts everybody involved. It's hard for me to say, but I know it's true. Their attempts to help should be of some comfort to you, even if they are misguided. Don't be afraid to reach out and ask for help. Staying in a rut when somebody can help you is foolish pride. One thing I have learned about being schizoaffective is to ask for help when I need it. Help does not jump out at you. Ask you if you need it.

I am not in the least saying that people can turn your day around. I am saying that there is a better chance of getting out of a rut through interaction with other people. There is a big difference. Some might say I am mincing words, but I will stand by them. For example, your problems are not going to change, and Johnny isn't going to make it right. So staying locked in a room with no interaction just allows you to wallow in your misery. This backs up my first statement. Now turn it around. Say you get out and run across Mrs. X, and she offers you a tomato because you seem a little peaked. It doesn't solve your problem, but you just might feel better.

Listen to me. I am the first one to logically state I know what I just wrote. I don't follow my own advice. I do just sit home and think bad thoughts more often than I should. I don't even watch uplifting television shows like *Dr. Phil* or *Rachael Ray* (my favorite). For me, writing works, because it is like getting outside. I think there are so many things to do inside with my words. I also get out on many a day and greet my customers. I may be playing the justification game, but in all honesty, I have nowhere to go. I also think I have too much to do around the house. Then I turn it around and play the tape of what I said in the last paragraph, or even at the start of this chapter, and my mental process of staying preoccupied begins. That is my recipe for a day. It is not a flawless theory or process, but it is one that helps. I am quite sure a professional would blow this right apart. I have to be honest and say that fifty years is a long time to settle into "habits." The sooner I kick out the bad ones, the better I will be, and I know writing is a good one for me.

So you might choose a habit wisely for the days that are dull, rainy, drab, or depressed. It might make the bad times go a lot better. I can't promise you that it will make all your problems go away (unless you need money and choose a profitable hobby). But I can almost assuredly say that you will be better off. Don't forget, you might incorporate a pet or two into your life. They can give you unconditional love and show you how to give it to yourself and them. That is just another day in my search for a Vivid Blue.

Chapter 29. There Are Two Sides to Every Coin

When a person is diagnosed with a disorder, it is usually because of apparent behavior issues. On average, the people he deals with on a daily basis know there is something wrong. The trained eye sees it for what it really is, while the less educated (for lack of a better description) just see a problem and cannot decipher the cause. They focus on the symptom most of the time and possibly even place blame in various inaccurate ways. It stands to reason that a person could assume any number of things about mental illness, and stories or past experiences make for a considerable barrier to overcome. It is no wonder mental illness carries a devastating stigma. If you can help it at all, you don't let your problems carry over into another's life. My schizoaffective problems have me feeling like I am at a disadvantage, or maybe even am condemned to a less than fortunate life, but to show it in my actions would be unacceptable. Oh, I am not going to say I haven't done that, because I have. It goes with the territory. At my worst, my actions were directed at the doctors who were trying to help me. I screamed foul in the doctor's office many times, and accused them of not working together in my best interest. I finally got the medicine that made me calm down, and then it got better. It wasn't until after I made a complete fool of myself that it turned around. It is more than a little embarrassing to admit I bit the hands of people who were trying to help me. I did, in my defense, have multiple problems, not just mental illness issues. As the saying goes, old age is no place for sissies, and I had a major physical ailment that threw a curveball into the mess.

I have a little story that illustrates how you should deal with other people and how you will get the same kind of response in return.

I lost my wallet, and subsequently I freaked out about it. I could have immediately assumed somebody stole my billfold, but I didn't take it to that extreme. Rarely do I think something so direct will happen to me, even though I have been hijacked in the past. What I didn't realize was that I had dropped it at the exact moment I thought it was missing. I knew my whole world was inside that little leather billfold. It was easier to lose because was smaller than the ones I have used before. I liked this new size because I could keep it in my front pocket. Anyway, I went for days without my wallet. In the meantime, I got both gas and cash from my father. That's when the real fun began. Actually, borrowing the money was easy. Paying it back was difficult.

I found my wallet after a couple of days while playing with my cats. I was lucky—it was just before I got a new driver's license, and only a day after I ordered my new Discover card. I still had to pay my dad back the money I borrowed. We agreed that the simplest thing to do was transfer the money directly from my account to his account. Since we have the same bank, we used their online services.

I logged on, checked my balance, and proceeded to transfer the money. I went through the normal process and typed in the correct numbers. It seemed to go through. I got a message that read, "Your account information will appear in the other member's account statement." I was finished—or so I thought.

With a few quick keystrokes, I bounced over to the summary page and waited for the money to be withdrawn. It never happened. My dad waited on the phone and asked me politely, "Did you send it?" Then he said, perplexed, "I didn't get it." It was a rare occurrence because the bank's site was usually pretty quick. This had never happened before. We waited for what seemed to be an ample amount of time, but the deposit never appeared.

Reluctantly, I filled out the information again. I double-checked the account number, amount, and the account holder's name. I proceeded to transfer the money. This was the second time. Naturally, I had some reservations about the process. I transferred the money, and once again the transfer never took place. My father told me, "I didn't get it," and I insisted that I'd sent it. Well, we deduced that the bank's system must have been down for the day. Dad said owing him for one more day wasn't going to hurt. We shut down our computers and said our goodbyes. We knew we would take care of this tomorrow.

The next afternoon rolled around and I called to tell my dad the deposits had indeed been lost in the ether. I told him I would immediately take care of it and that I was sorry for the mix-up. Of course, my dad said he understood. I made the transfer. It said, "Your account information will appear in the other member's account statement." I was finished. I immediately switched over to my account information page and checked to see if the money had been withdrawn. Nope. The money still hadn't transferred. I couldn't believe it. Now I was frustrated. I began to think it was my computer. Rather than fix my computer on the spot, which might not be the right thing to do, I decided to do a test. I switched computers.

I went into my office and started the process on my desktop. This was to be the ultimate test. Nothing ever goes wrong with this computer. I never use it. It is essentially pristine. Once again, I painstakingly entered the information. Needless to say, I was tired of doing this. As you probably expect, it didn't work. Immediately I concluded that it was the bank's problem. That was when I thought somebody might be tampering with my account. I had to overrule this idea and move on with my day. Ultimately I wondered what was up with the bank's website. Since it was the weekend, I would wait until Monday and call the bank.

On Monday I called. I wasn't perturbed and I didn't even have to wait a long time. The automated system said I was the next caller in line. When it was my turn, a sprightly young voice chirped, "This is Ashley, may I help you?"

"Yes, Ashley, I have a problem," I said. I explained my problem in great detail, making sure not to leave anything out. I told her the computer did indeed say the transfer had been made. I wasn't sure how they wanted to pursue this, but the ball was now in their court. Then she asked me all the pertinent questions, like my name and account number, to confirm I was the account holder. After the formalities were established, we started to correct the problem.

Ashley then asked me to go through the steps once again, but this time she wanted me to explain what I was doing. I did. I carefully, consistently, and methodically went over each step. I detailed each one. I came up with the same error. She said, "That's okay." Evidently she had expected it. She was just doing her job. Then she asked me to go through the steps again. By this time I was no stranger to the process, so I very quickly filled out the information. I made sure I told her every step so that she knew I wasn't leaving anything out. The same message popped up: "Your account information will appear in the other member's account statement." I was terribly frustrated, but I didn't let her know. There are some things you don't do in this world, and one of them is make somebody on the phone bear the brunt of all your problems. Besides, I still wanted to know as much about the problem as she did.

We ended up trying it a couple more times, with the same results. During this time, we chatted. She was a delightful girl, and I remarked that a few years ago, I had worked the help desk at the Corps of Engineers. I told her I loved that job. She said she loved hers too. She said she loved hearing people talk about their lives, and that when she fixed a problem, she got a great sense of satisfaction. I told her my current job was essentially the same. We were making this ill-fated venture fun. We were not, however, making progress. Finally she said, "I have to call for support." She didn't know what to do anymore. This was beyond her scope. She had never encountered a problem like this.

She put me on hold for a minute or two, and then came back and said, "They tried it on their end and it worked."

"How can that be?" I asked, perplexed. "How did they do that?"

"Let's try it one more time," she said. I did, and got the same message: "Your account information will appear in the other member's account statement." Then she asked, "What does the next screen say?"

I stuttered for a long second and said, "What next screen?"

"The one after that message."

I told her there was no next screen, that I just popped over to accounts and checked my balance. She told me to read everything on that page carefully. I read out loud the bold red line that said, "Your account information will appear in the other member's account statement." There was a long pause, and then I was forced to say, "I'm supposed to hit the 'confirm transfer' button, aren't I?" I decided I probably shouldn't tell her about losing my wallet.

I realized it wasn't okay to take my frustrations out on somebody else. I was so glad I hadn't acted in rage from the beginning, because it would have been so wrong. As a matter of fact, it would have doubled my embarrassment. I admit, that wasn't the exact moment I realized it. It just backed up everything I knew to be true. Sure, there was a time when I was younger when I didn't handle myself properly. Actually, somewhere in the past, I learned rage was an effective way to look like a complete ass. The Vivid Blue saga was sprawled out for all to see when I noticed it the least. It took years to control my emotions, and even more time to logically put my disorders out where I could control them. Most of my progress was made when I faced my demons. I saw myself as normal and entitled, and I really was the last to see the reality of being a human with disorders. That was a hard sentence to write, and I think it was just as hard to absorb as this book. So to the many people who suffer, I say don't attach such weight to the judgment portion of the disorder, and spend your time and effort thinking about ways you can better deal with it. How you interact with other people does say a lot about you, and how your disorder affects others should be a primary focus. Naturally we fall short at times, but this is an opportunity to do better. That is what my search for a Vivid Blue has taught me.

Chapter 30. How Can You Tell If You Are Making Progress?

All too often I wonder what my life would be like if I had done things a little differently. I pick out one signature event from my past and then extrapolate all the things I think would follow. I go back as far as I can and play the what-if game until my mind is overloaded with hypothetical scenarios. Almost invariably I go down paths that are wanton dreams of better choices. I look at the decisions that I made and think I could have done better. I ask myself, "Why did I do that?" Most of the reasons were justifiable at the time. I tell myself it would happen again unless I knew then what I know now. That is always the key. What I know now has evolved. I like to think I have gotten smarter as I have progressed into each new decade. I must assume I am no different than anybody else in this regard. It is when rubber hits the pavement that I have it different than the average "normal" person. I have to deal with all the regrettable things in my past that can only be chalked up to my schizoaffective disorder. For this I'm supposed to learn and keep my head up. However, I cannot change it. On the other hand, I feel like I should be able to change my OCD and PTSD.

I knew it was wrong of me to state so emphatically that I would do things differently based on "knowing then what I know now." Of course I would. Saying that doesn't give any credibility to the fact that my disorders play out in the ever-so-distasteful manner they do. Just having schizoaffective disorder, OCD, and PTSD implies that there are certain things I cannot control. The word "imply" doesn't even cover it—I should use words like "mandate" or "force." Somehow these words seem more appropriate; they are the real definition. I want to come up with any and every possible way of explaining how these disorders hold me hostage. I like to think I am a great negotiator too. I make all sorts of compromises just dealing with my circumstances. Just taking my medications is a compromise. Yes, boohoo. I have to take my meds. That is the least uncomfortable part of the equation. Then there is the slew of negative thoughts I must battle. For one thing, I have to deal with my memories of my past indiscretions. For example, I have to deal with how to make it past the neighbor I insulted by telling him his fence looked bad. I didn't phrase it as nicely, either. Funny thing, I think the fence still looks bad. I just wish I hadn't marched up to his front door and told him to his face. I know it sounds bad that I would do something so awful. In my defense, the fence was within perfect sight of my living room, with the building slats facing out. On top of that, the fence had been built crooked by half-assed carpenters. I was mad, and am still mad. I am reminded of it every day, and of my bad behavior. This isn't the only thing I have done, either. I have all sorts of little and big things that add up to a schizoaffective nightmare. What's worse is I promptly stewed about it obsessively with my OCD until I wasn't mad about the fence but instead became mad at my own behavior. When I realized that the only thing I could have done about the whole thing was just accept it and do nothing, I had to ask myself, "Was this really part of my disorder, or was it me blaming my disorder?" It was in the past. In order to prevent it from reoccurring, I had to answer that question.

The knowledge I have learned about myself is one of the things that ties me so closely to my disorders. I know knowledge and actions are two different things altogether. My doctors are able to discover a pattern, yet I am unable to see it. They want to help, they try to help, but they are only armed with pills and words. That is a callous thing to say, and I will go even farther and say my attitude in this regard is just plain wrong unless you were strictly going by how a SABP person feels. Yet still, my problem is more serious than pills or words can address. I have no way of conveying my feelings and emotions other than to verbalize them, and that is lacking. I am armed with medications and the knowledge that spills over from the doctors. Any other knowledge is subjective and is often discredited for obvious reasons. By the way, I am not confident in my medications or in my knowledge. I bide my time, hoping that my feelings will not become too strong. We all know what happens to somebody who can't handle his problems. So on good days, I fight my demons by myself, and on bad days, I only talk to the few people

I trust. I survive without ever letting the majority of my friends know what is really going on. My disorders do a number on me, and I work with whatever cards I have. I always think pills and words are not enough. When I have a meltdown, I think, was this part of my disorder, or was it a bad temper tantrum? In the case of my neighbor's fence, it was a bad temper tantrum. It was probably caused by everything hitting at once. I can start to explain why I went into the hospital, and why it was during a depressed moment. Well, there I go again, a justification. How do I reconcile my past without using justifications? It sounds the same. I can explain almost everything bad in my past and it sounds like a horror story. Events keep happening and they are in the recent past, not just the distant past. So the ultimate question, the question of all questions, is: How do I know if I have made any progress at all?

We ask ourselves the same questions in society, but society is a little different. We seem doomed to repeat the same mistakes. Wait, maybe we're just like society. Society progresses slowly as a whole, and it takes decades for improvements to become manifest. Just the other day, I was on a blog and saw people's reaction to homosexuals. They were still saying the same old things. One said he would teach his boys to beat up homosexuals, while another said gays were why God created AIDS. The lack of intelligence was astounding and sad. Wouldn't God have wanted the Christians to act like Christians? I felt like we hadn't made any progress since the '80s, yet there are examples like the president moving us in positive directions with his inclusion of gay issues in his speeches. What other signs tell us we are progressing? What would it mean if the next president reversed the actions of his or her predecessor? Clearly we go back and forth with our progress, in stages that seem longer than any single individual can impact. In mental illness, I think we are progressing. We just aren't progressing fast enough.

When do we realize we have made a personal achievement, then? What do we look for as clues that signify a benchmark of our overall success? If we were cutting the grass, we would see a finely trimmed lawn. But that doesn't work for mental illness. For schizoaffective people, it would mean there were no "schizo" moments and certainly no manic or depressed moments. So we are back to the same question: How do we tell if we have made any progress? It is all subjective and up to the individual. The person has to see signs of it in actions, behaviors, or attitudes. If it could be all three, it would be ideal. Oh, such a simple answer. That doesn't even begin to relate to the measurement or even address how we would quantify such progress. What would our benchmarks be? We couldn't dare compare ourselves with others in the same boat. Time is definitely the biggest factor.

The first turning point for me was a physical sign. I never saw a sign until late in my diagnosis (treatment), and I still work to convince myself that things are better. Maybe it always going to be that way, and maybe everybody associated with schizoaffective disorder is the same way. I am not writing about the definition of schizoaffective disorder, I am writing about my dealings with my disorders. Anyway, the first thing I noticed was an action: I stopped chewing my fingernails. I was in my late forties, and I had been chewing my nails since my before my teens. I didn't even know how I stopped. I went to a new doctor, and I went into the hospital. I got a new diagnosis and new meds. Boom, I stopped chewing my nails. It seemed like a miracle. I had the hardest time believing it and went around telling everybody who would listen. It didn't change my mood swings. It had nothing to do with my paranoia, but clearly my OCD was better. Another thing was I stopped buying all that ridiculous glass. My medication was working like it should, and my OCD was better. I was still OCD. I obsessed about things like the land I was selling or about my paranoia, but not nearly as much. Unfortunately, I still grind my teeth.

After I noticed my marked improvement, I started to ask myself the bigger questions. Why wasn't my life working like it should? I kept thinking my life was a wreck. I used that term a lot too. "Wreck" was a word I liked to use. It implied something big, as in train wreck or airplane crash. I was going to need answers to a lot of questions before it was all over. Still, there is the one remaining question: How do I tell if I am doing better? The only sign as of yet was physical. It wasn't enough that I stopped chewing my fingernails, because I was still going through mood swings that were affecting my life. I can hate being schizoaffective all day, but it wasn't going to change. I could pray and it wasn't going to change. It seemed I could take my medications and it wasn't going to change. I am hopelessly schizoaffective, and yet I was still looking for signs that I was making progress.

Some things in life are right under our own noses. Maybe we like to use the phrase "can't see the forest for the trees." For me, I was hoping it would be right there. But it wasn't at all. There was a relief from OCD—and oh, wait. I did notice one more thing, but it doesn't have anything to do with my schizoaffective disorder. My attention span was longer than it's been since college. I was thinking more clearly and with less resistance, if you will. Could I have my own little answer? I could write for hours, and this time I was making more sense. As a matter of fact, I didn't have to go back and rewrite with the intent of making my ideas or thought processes clear. I could write and not have to erase whole sentences or paragraphs. I wasn't putting in things that had no bearing on my initial thought. I don't know when the change occurred. It didn't matter when it happened, either, because that wasn't the point. I planned on running with the ball.

My only problems now are daily things and, over time, my mood swings. I still fall prey to days when I sink into really bad depressions. Now I manage to tell myself that I was "clearly" depressed or manic. I use my own little terms against myself whenever I can. I know I shouldn't, but I am so sarcastic. My medications for mood swings aren't working like the OCD medications have, and I expected a miracle. It wasn't fair, either. I was happiest when I was manic and a new piece of glass came in the mail. Forget the fact that I couldn't afford it. I would trade my depression for a piece of new treasure. Of course, when I was manic, everything was fine except the checkbook and the cocky little attitude everybody hated.

Then there was the realization: I wasn't looking out the window or waiting for the door to be kicked in. That was what I needed for my little sign. Actually, it was a huge sign. I could go for an hour at first, then for maybe two. I was finally getting some relief. I knew I wasn't doing anything wrong and that my actions didn't warrant any attention by officials, or by anyone, for that matter. I had logically come to that point where I knew emotionally I didn't feel that way. Now it was better. Now I was making progress.

Working on staying positive is harder than anything at any given time. I can say things must give the appearance of improving. I know I am not in the terrible place I was in emotionally when I went into the hospital. For that I am grateful. It is all about perspective. I wake in the morning knowing I have a feeling that is still beyond my control. I take my meds to deal. I hope they will work better in time. It's pretty simple, really. Do it again tomorrow and voila, you have a recipe for handling your life. Oh, why can't it work like my OCD medications? Well, I still have hope. If meds worked like that for my OCD, then things can work for my schizoaffective disorder. There is still hope I will find the right medications, or someone will invent one that works better. There is progress because I am handling my circumstances better. On the other hand, my comprehension is still not what it used to be when I was in college. That is a side effect of the medication.

For years I have waited for the future to unfold. I am sure that sounds weird, but I stand by what I say. It is like gambling. I waited until I got out of my parents' house. I waited to get both my high school and college degrees. I waited until the medication worked. It was always wait. Now I don't have enough time in my life to wait for a new wave of medication, yet the disorders still have me captive, so wait I must. I know I am doing better with my OCD, and that gives me hope. Not enough time has elapsed since my last episode for me to think I have made the same progress with my schizoaffective disorder. That doesn't mean I haven't been progressing, though, it just means I have to be patient. The fact that I acknowledge my need for patience is progress in itself. I think I will do better next time; therefore I will.

Overall, though, since I got out of the hospital, I have learned to control my delusions. I can logically think my way past certain situations. I don't fall prey to things that would have tripped me up two or three years ago. So yes, over a long stretch of time (time being the factor), I have made progress. There is another thing to consider, and that is that my coping skills get stronger as days pass. I no longer think everybody in a truck outside my house is about to break in and steal some important document. I logically think my documents (medical records, etc.) are of no importance and that anybody who would go to that much trouble would get them by some other means. I have made progress, and I haven't needed to go to a therapist or talk to somebody to alleviate my worry. I also logically think it is not right to have any of these thoughts in the first place. I force myself to think of something totally different. Then I try to plan what to do with the remainder of the day, week, or month, etc. I find that planning something is positive for me. That is, as long as I plan something positive.

There are certain things I can control very well, like anger issues. For example, I was in Arby's recently, and the attendant was being berated by the guy right in front of me. I was getting very upset and kept thinking he shouldn't be doing that. I went from being angry to wanting to do something. With a decisive but controlled manner, I didn't act. In my mind, I wanted the man to feel physically what he was making the attendant feel emotionally. Before I said anything, the manager stepped in and took over. The customer never stopped with his attitude, and I immediately thought to myself, "What kind of messed-up life do you have to have to take your frustrations out on somebody else? What kind of life do you have to make people feel bad when they are trying to help you?" My thought processes weren't incorrect that day. They were just normal human responses to a bad situation. The more I think about it, the more I am proud I didn't do something. I would have overreacted in an escalating manner, and something bad would have come from it. That would have been wrong.

The biggest sign of progress can be seen in interactions with other people. It isn't as simple as a smile returning a smile. There are other things to consider, like the way you carry yourself, or the ways you start a conversation. If people are always nervous or anxious around you, then you need to analyze what you are doing so that you can eliminate your part of the equation. Monitoring your own actions is imperative. For example, my phone went out the other day. I called and made an appointment with the phone company. They said they would have somebody out to fix it the next day, if I could keep my schedule open and let the technician in when he arrived. I readily agreed because I needed my phone and could rearrange my plans. By the next afternoon, the technician hadn't shown up yet, so I called. The person I spoke to said there wasn't an appointment. I got upset. I didn't take it out on the service person, but I did stomp around the house and scare my cats into hiding. It wasn't my cats' fault, and yet they were paying the price. It took a little while for me to sit down and for one of them to come out. Then I realized that my actions are guiding things that happen to me. Sometimes my actions are really small, but what if I did something big like setting somebody off at the Department of Motor Vehicles, and as a result they didn't want to help me? What if I scared somebody because of my schizoaffective behavior, which could easily be the case? Chances are they would shy away from being my friend. I don't want people to think I'm a bad guy, because I'm not. They can't tell just by looking at me that there is a schizoaffective person inside a normal human shell. I have to analyze my behaviors and correct what I portray incorrectly. I don't expect it to be easy. As a matter of fact, I expect it to be hard. It will be a sign of my progress.

Learning to gauge your own body's progress is a must when you have a chronic mental illness. It isn't as easy as pulling yourself aside and going down a checklist of symptoms and behaviors. You must analyze your overall well-being by accessing your logic and thought processes. The search for a Vivid Blue has kept me under the microscope. It has been a worthwhile endeavor and a necessary one to promote self-healing. My overall progress has been good, and for that I am thankful.

Chapter 31. Where Do I Go from Here?

This general abstract was written in a day and polished up within just a few hours before I decided to put it into my book. It seemed to fit right here magically, and it seems to be calling out to anybody who has ever wanted to quit, throw in the towel, or take even more drastic measures to solve their plights. I believe there are many reasons to take your medications, even if you think they aren't working or are not the right ones. Don't give up. The most resounding proof can be found in simple little tasks around the house. One such story that always rings true is in my yard. I sigh with a usual grunt every spring on yard day. It is the day I dedicate at the beginning of the year to keeping my forest tame. I don't do a good job of keeping up my lawn, and it shows. It is a time-consuming and very mundane task. I don't entirely dislike it, but I do dislike getting started because of petty little nagging feelings, two of which are "Where do I begin?" and "When will my back start hurting?" Yes, to the older clan, it's a resounding "You are too young to have back problems"; to the younger folk, it is some form of "I cannot relate." There is a song in there somewhere, but then again, who cares? I know to move past the pain and finish the lawn.

The same analogy can be applied to my whole life, and I wonder if it isn't something most everybody goes through. At some point one must wake up and smell the coffee, be it good or bad. We can be logical or spiritual, or the act can be random or accidental, but however it happens, we must come to the conclusion that we all wake from our youth into another form of existence. It happens around the time you start getting called ma'am or sir. Yes, youth ends and maturity will flow completely through our veins. This maturity will guide us into making decisions that require more forethought, and this same maturity shows us the consequences of our bad decisions. Over the years, this process gives us wisdom and experience. I wonder if it is truly lucky to have been sheltered and remain knock free until life hits hard. Maybe it's the ones who get knocked hard in the beginning who find the most peace. I think, contrary to a few isolated events, that I am the former, with the attitude of the latter. Maybe it will save me from all that life can truly dish out, but I suspect it can't and it won't. Life is a four-letter word, and even though I have made it through quite a bit, most of what has transpired has just been preparing me for the next wave.

The predominant thing on my mind is "Where do I go from here?" Life surely has the keys to a myriad of locks. It isn't as simple as choosing a door, because that would be an easy way of justifying what has happened or transpired. Instead we are whisked away down a river at breakneck speed, hoping to open the floodgate before the water backs up, and we drown in a proverbial pool of life's predicaments. Quite often we think we survived because God was looking out for us, and most of the time we are right. So once again I ask, "Where do I go from here?" Well, "I don't know" might just be an answer. Yet "I don't know" will not suffice. There are no luxuries as an adult facing the real future. Tomorrow brings what it will, and just as it can bring joy, it can also bring sorrow.

I have to be pragmatic and say not all my plans have been thwarted every step of the way. From the tragedy of my best friend's murder to the great success of running my own business, I have made it here without a clue of what the future would hold. I will say the only things I did have control over were things like solidarity with my family and friends. I too will go down with the ship. I am intelligent enough to see that where I plan to go isn't necessarily where I will be in the end. I can say the important things are right in my heart and in my intent. I know my choices will be the right ones when they pertain to my loved ones. I hope my choices for myself will end up being correct too. I have made it halfway, and I am looking forward to the next half. I do plan on a bright future, but I also plan for that occasional rainy day that shall come too. So I must ask that question one more time: Where do I go from here? I must get an answer. It must be a satisfying answer, one that will suffice for the rest of my life. So where will my Vivid Blue take me? To answer anything less than "All the way!" would not be satisfactory.

Chapter 32. Life Gets Better as We Get Older

For most people, age marks an improvement of the mindset. As we get older, we learn. As we learn, we realize we know very little about everything in general. We also realize that nobody else has the answers, so we humbly try to fix our own little problems and not cause too many for the ones we love. For people with schizoaffective disorder, though, life doesn't work that way. There will always be an aspect that is uncontrollable, even with medicine. I learned that I couldn't count on my body being the same day after day. This I learned without ever being told. I look back over the years and think of my dysfunctional life. When my doctor first told me I had a mental disorder, I never thought to relate that to my past. I guess I wasn't that bright, or maybe there was too much information to digest. Either way, I didn't make the correlation. Now that I have accepted my disorders, it only seems logical that I would look back and try to see the dysfunctional points. Not only did the schizoaffective problems have me going from one extreme to another, OCD had me thinking cyclically about my problems. How did I survive? How do I sort out the many fiascos that can only be attributed to my disorder? My past is my past, and I can't change it. I did have a few good things happen, though. I did graduate college, after all. I did accomplish some pretty lofty goals despite my disorders. I know now it is because I kept on trying. I have begun to realize life gets better as we get older.

Now, as I progress into my later years, I look back at life with the added benefit of more experience. I have made mistakes that I will never forget, and as a result, I have become more cautious. I am less likely to have the same pitfalls trip me up. Since I know what my diagnosis is, I feel ready to tackle my problems. I know I have beat this drum to death, but before the diagnosis, you cope, and after the diagnosis, you can manage. It is never easy to come to grips with your disorders. But the sooner you do so, the sooner you can build self-awareness in your life. It took me years to accept my disorders, and that made the struggle long and arduous. I fought the doctors and I changed doctors. I did everything I could to avoid believing that I had a disorder. I went from what I thought was depression to bipolar and then onto schizoaffective. Every step of the way, I had to learn more about myself. I also made many mistakes and had many outbursts. I took my anger out on my friends and my family. There were times I blew up at my neighbors. Needless to say, I did things that were very hard to control at the time. Over the years I became more adjusted to the medicines and learned to accept life. The disorders became the norm, but so did the treatment. Sure, I feel owned by them, but my confidence in making it through life has become greater. I can handle it now. I have a greater sense of awareness.

There is another key thing that I want to mention about awareness. You don't have to make comparisons anymore. Your journey is your own, and where you are in life has no bearing on anybody else's life. You don't need to apologize to anybody for your shortcomings. If others think you are falling short, then they don't understand all you're going through. That is it, period. The reverse is true too. If you are thinking that you should be doing as well as so-and-so, but you're not, give yourself a break and quit comparing. You don't know what other people are going through or what their walk of life is all about. I would bet their life isn't easy. My best friend's mom always said to me, "Everybody has as much as they can handle." How you treat yourself has everything to do with how you feel. It took me years to figure this one out, and I still struggle with it. I sometimes think my disorders mean I have a death sentence and that my friends get to live a normal life. I have to back myself out of that thinking very consciously and methodically until I get to the point where I am happy again. I also have to quit thinking subconsciously that I must be stupid because "I blew myself up." I don't even know I am thinking that way, yet I have to reverse the thought process. I have to rely on the medication to stop the OCD too. It is working.

I am certain that the older I get, the more relaxed I get, due to confidence in decision making. I seem to have a better track record, and I get better feedback from loved ones. I know to stick with my medications. I know to get proper sleep. I know that the company I

190

keep will lead to either headaches or peace. It doesn't have to be the blatantly obvious choices, either. I can tell when it is better to do something a certain way, like baking something in the oven with a slow, even heat, instead of heating it up quickly and consequently burning it. My disorders are complicated, just like anybody else's, and I now have more ammo to fight them. I like it when I have made the right choice. It prepares me mentally to do it again. When I don't make the right choice, I have enough experience to know I will do better next time.

My disorders have left me thinking I would be better off if I didn't take chances. My overly cautious behavior has always been a double-edged sword. There is the old saying "You can sit on the sidelines all day and watch the world pass you by." I was "the boy who blew himself up," and I learned very early that actions have consequences. You can't let your disorders stop you. I had to tell myself that multiple times in order to believe it, and only after years did it start to work. That really was the case of life getting better as we get older. Getting older helped me realize which opportunities were worth the risk too. It is called experience, and it only comes from making decisions. Both good and bad decisions teach us to do better the next time. A proper diagnosis helps us make better choices. It takes years after the diagnosis to realize that you have been operating with incorrect information in terms of what to tackle and what to avoid. When we know more about ourselves (and that takes a lot of time), we can apply that knowledge with experience and start to develop healthy habits. Making the right decisions becomes crucial. This adds stress to the process, and getting older relieves some of that importance. For me, getting older relieved some of that fear. I adopted the attitude that "whatever will be, will be."

I may have discovered my disorders late in life, but when I finally came to terms with them, things gradually became better. This was due to having the right medications and the right mindset. I also noticed a correlation between the better mindset and the better class of people. It was obvious I was beginning to hang around people who were more intelligent, more compassionate, and more understanding. I have to stress one point: I have always said the people in your life matter. You also need to determine if they are pulling you down. The only way to really know this comes from experience and time. You need to gather information about how they treat you over the long haul. Did they really just slight you? For me, I put it into another context altogether. Did I want them as friends in the first place? Did I really want to hang around them? Life got a lot better when I weeded out the people who were keeping me in the same old places. It is my choice whom I hang with. I have all the power necessary to control what I cultivate. I will always remember hearing that Maya Angelou would walk up to and politely ask you to leave one of her parties if you used inappropriate language. I may not be that strict about language, but I will weed you out of my life if you are a put-down artist.

The relationships we build with ourselves and others are the best part of getting older. For people with schizoaffective disorder, cultivating this is a difficult process. It is for me, anyway. My paranoia and self-esteem get in the way of my progress. I cannot begin to explain the magnitude of damage I did to my own psyche over blowing myself up. But my true friends don't care or make me explain. As I get older, they just seem to take me as I am. My mistakes seem to go along for the ride. I am a complete package. They still accept me, as I do them. By the way, I don't keep up with their mistakes, so I am willing to bet they are not keeping up with mine. I have to remind myself all the time that I shouldn't be keeping score of my mistakes, except to learn from them. I shouldn't be telling myself I am dumb or stupid. I have to correct these bad habits in order to continue with my life and not go down a destructive path. It's true, I have been the hardest on myself. Getting older made me realize it, and it gives me the opportunity to change it at the same time. Life really does get better as we get older.

By opening our minds to the possibility that life gets better, we allow for good things to happen. It is a positive, forward mindset that can only bring good things. The self-fulfilling negativity that follows bad thoughts should be enough to keep you away from them. Negativity is a crippling part of the disorder. I fall into that rut too many times. Knowing that it is a problem and then learning (over time) ways to combat this demon is a key part of the fight. I have been lucky enough to go to a group meeting where I met others who have schizoaffective disorder, and I listened to the ways they handled their situations. I incorporated some of their wisdom and methods, and it has made me stronger. I didn't try them all, and of course I had the option of deciding (over time) which ones really worked.

I am always happiest for people who get their diagnosis early, when they can actually work on their behavior patterns. I am sad they have a disorder. But the sooner they come out of denial, the sooner they can begin their journey to a healthier way of life. I will always wonder what life would have been like if I had gotten counseling for my burns and subsequently for my schizoaffective disorder. Life got better as I got older anyway, but think what would have happened if I'd had a jump start. Maybe I would have gotten my degree at twenty-four instead of twenty-eight. Who knows? Anyway, it isn't healthy to go down this path of regret. I am very grateful I didn't go my whole life without help. That would have been a shame, especially since help is there. Staying quiet or ignoring the signs is the wrong thing to do.

For chronically mentally ill people, our situation will go in ebbs and tides. Through enough of these fluctuations, the patterns will arise and the philosophy of "this too shall pass" can take hold. I still go through wild extremes, and it shows in my writing. One day I will write the most optimistic thing you could ever read, and then the very next day I will write about how the world is the worst place ever. I try to find a happy medium, one that I believe in. Through it all, I still find that the book gets better the farther along I get. I have to hope the two extremes will iron themselves out with time. I do believe my life has gotten better as I have gotten older. The realization of this little tidbit has illuminated a unique philosophy for my search. My Vivid Blue would not be complete without recognition of all the things that make life better. It does take time to sort it out.

Chapter 33. Making Myself Happy

It is important to have people to look up to during times of great stress. For me, that's my father. He has a way of moving forward through any disaster. Many times in my life, I've wondered how he does it. I guess there must be a fatherly instinct that never lets the son know the fear. My father's fear of mental illness must be enormous. I really can't guess what he goes through, but I know that he is still proud, even if he has a hard time accepting my disorders. I really can't do anything to make another person deal with his or her hang-ups. Therefore I must simply help myself, no matter how selfish that sounds.

I would like to take a moment to say I am not being callous. I am in no way telling you to just get over it. I know life doesn't work that way. You have to confront your problems head on. Please don't read anything trite into what I am saying, because I do believe there are problems that can and should consume you, as well as problems with chemical imbalances that cannot be corrected by words. Please forgive my lack-minded statements in advance when I present a "little philosophy" that may or may not work for you. I have many days when this load doesn't even come close to helping me, but I try.

On the days I feel like making the effort, the process I go through to find happiness is both simple and complex. When it works right, it is the simplest thing in the world. I wish that for anyone who reads this chapter. When I try and don't reach my goal, I get frustrated and fall apart. Hopefully we won't have to go there. Anyway, these are steps I take to make myself happy. Simple as it may be, it is a two-part formula. The two parts are 1) say what I want out loud, and 2) forget the details until it happens. Both parts are crucial to the formula. Both parts seem like a load of crap until you try it. There, I said it. I agree with you. It sounds like I am so full of it, and I hate writing it too, because half the time I don't believe it either. The fact remains, however, that the conscious effort must be made, and sometimes I have to remind myself of that. It takes work to achieve this far-fetched goal. I can tell you that you must figure out a way to get past forgetting to do this. Remember, whatever you do, you have to do the whole process once completely before you believe it works. I know it will help.

First, it is easier to be happy if you affirm the goal. There is some sort of mental preparedness that goes on when you do this step. Saying it out loud sounds dumb, but it etches it in stone, if you will. I am no expert on the human mind, but I am sure this trick has been documented. If I look in the mirror in the morning and say out loud, "It's going to be a good day," most of the time it will be a good day. It is even better if you can say, "It is going to be a great day." When I first moved into my house back in 2003, I had an experience that was quite memorable. I walked into my kitchen and saw the cutest little bird on the back deck. I told it, "Yes, it's going to be a great day." Without even realizing what I was doing or saying, I spoke to a little bird. Was I going nuts? I don't think so. I continued making my morning coffee, and then I realized what I had told the bird. At least that was what I thought happened. I couldn't stop thinking about it. I had just answered a bird. Did it even matter? All that mattered now was that I had a good day. It was a great day.

The second part of forgetting about something until it happens is true too. If you stay focused on the here and now, you are too tied to your problems. This is where I fail most of the time. I am sure most if not all depressed people will balk at the thought of just saying that it will be a good day and then expecting it to happen. That isn't exactly what I'm saying, and that isn't where the concept fails either. It fails when the depression or circumstance is so bad that you can't shake it long enough to forget about it. If you can forget about being depressed, lonely, sad, or whatever, it becomes more likely you will be able to trick your mind into believing you're happy. You can't stay consumed by the bad day. Well, you can, and quite easily I'm sure. I'm willing to bet everybody has more than enough to handle, and some have more than two people can handle. With my OCD, I stayed consumed with whatever was wrong. Now I am learning to shift my thoughts away from the main problem. If the problem is the car making a bad noise, I try to think, it wouldn't matter if I were at the beach. If I have to pay $1600 to fix a tooth, I try to remember that there are people who would love to be able to get their teeth fixed. If I cannot afford anything during this hopefully short interrupt, I think harder to find things that are my blessings. I am not being calloused. Somehow I try to offset my problem, and then hopefully I can let it go completely. It didn't work that way for my kidney stone. I had to have three procedures (two and the stent removal). The stent was all I could think about. It made the time agonizingly slow. Anyway, if I could have let it go completely, I would have been able to acknowledge the "it is going to be a great day" part of my equation.

There is nothing better than a day that took care of itself. If I get to the end of the day and I didn't have to worry about something, then I've achieved my goal. I don't necessarily want to try to make the day go by faster, because I want the day to be more fun and therefore seem faster. The only time you should think about time is when it relates to an appointment. It took me most of my life to figure out that all I had to do was try to affirm my happiness. The concept doesn't come from any member of my family, so I am not sure where it fits into my search for a Vivid Blue. I do know that I will keep on trying to tell myself to be happy, because most of the time it works. For all you skeptics out there, just give it a try. You might find that it works too. If it only works one day out of the year, you're still better off, right? For you really negative people like me, don't you need this help with the other 364?

Chapter 34. Friends

What book would be complete without discussing friendships? Friendship requires a mutual respect formed by two or more parties with similar interests. It also requires cultivation and maintenance. That is not to say that it should be difficult, because it shouldn't. There is an art to both gaining and keeping a friend. I seem to be better at gaining a friend than keeping one. It is probably because of my big mouth. To remain true to yourself or your friends, you can't rehearse every line you say. At some point there must be uninhibited conversation. I often wonder about the moments when my friends don't agree with what I am saying. It occurs to me that they might be holding back their opinions. If by chance they go completely silent, then I wonder if they secretly might not want to hurt my feelings. My disorders give me a different perspective from most people's, and it is apparent that some people would find my oscillating outlook distasteful.

It is my perception that almost every aspect of my schizoaffective behavior tends to drive people away. For the most part, dealing with both schizoaffective and OCD behavior usually requires a higher intelligence. It definitely requires more experience and more tolerance. I would also think patience is a virtue too. I know my actions dealing with my "boy who blew himself up" complex can't be easily interpreted, and I am often misunderstood. Keeping my condition a secret means people never get to know me. By the same token, if I reveal too much information, I can sever a friendship. There are many situations in which people might be willing to be your friend but not know how to be friendly. They really don't know how to proceed. It takes a special kind of understanding to rise above my schizoaffective mood swings. The different actions of a schizoaffective person vary widely and cannot be predicted. It is a curse for which we have constantly sought help.

I look at my friendships differently as I get older. It would seem the people I haven't irritated or scared off are my true friends. All my friends are special to me, and all my friends deserve kudos. They stand tall as wonderful, generous beings. Some know about my disorders and some don't. The ones who don't might be even more receptive to my disorders because they have already accepted my faults without attributing a reason for them. I'm sure after this book gets out, all will know. I'm sure the ones who matter, the courageous ones, will still be my friends.

I look in the mirror and I seem harmless enough. I don't think I look like a person with a problem. I don't talk to myself or anything like that, but I do stand in front of the mirror and wonder what other people see. I especially wonder what the people who know about my disorders see. I hope they see someone who is determined to overcome his adversity. I hope they see somebody who is moving past his monumental mistakes and severe disorders.

I break my friendships into several groups: friends I made at work; the few lifelong friends that I haven't driven away; and the current friends who accept me. The rest are just acquaintances, and the qualities of my relationships with them may or may not rank on the scale of things I consider to be criteria of friendship.

Lifelong relationships are casualties of war when it comes to my schizoaffective diagnosis. These friends never knew they would be entering a war zone, either. It goes with the territory. Most of my lifelong friends know that they have to take my mood swings with a grain of salt. It is the paranoia they don't understand. I have to be careful and not share too much, because it will adversely affect everything. We are never guaranteed anything in life, and friends are among those things not guaranteed. Why do I say that? Because friendships can be destroyed. I have destroyed them by both action and neglect. Sometimes it was my friend's fault, but mostly it was mine. I have been good at it—so good I have perfected it. Also, a few of my friends choose not to return phone calls. Maybe they can't absorb the information, or maybe they don't know and merely perceive something. Maybe they just want to play it safe. Whatever the case, at times my friendships have strained the normal boundaries. There is a saying that I have adapted to my personal use that is very appropriate here: "You should not expect anything from anybody, and true friends should not expect anything from you." I have too great an expectation from far too many people for that saying not to apply to me. It is funny, though, I want to think of people like my cats: give them enough time and attention and they will end up being my friends.

When I get together with my friends, I choose to not overanalyze everything. Worrying about the details might start the conversation off on the wrong foot. I have the best of intentions, but my actions always undermine my integrity. Basically I have the actions of insecurity mixed with my opinion, and that spells disaster. The body language I use must be sour to a lot of people. It is an overcompensation for being "the boy who blew himself up" and for my paranoia. I really can't help it.

There was a time when my body told a truth I was completely embarrassed to disclose. This happened at work at my first job after graduation. I was beaten up by a bunch of thugs. The fight was over a rainbow sticker on the bumper of my new Integra. My face was black and blue, just like in the movies. All I really remember of the fight was that they tackled me and kept kicking me until I ran back to my car. During the scuffle they damaged the door. I went to work my first day, on my first job out of college, battered and bruised. What a sob story.

There is no telling what people think when you have the signs of being beaten up. The people who see you this way might think you deserved it. To some degree I did. I didn't know how to stay out of a fight. I had a rainbow sticker on the bumper of my car. I wasn't very streetwise. To top that off, I didn't want to make a police report. My father said that he would pay for the door to be repaired if I did make a report, and if I took off the rainbow sticker. It was blackmail. I live in the South. I decided there was no point in advertising. Besides, I had enough things going in all directions.

The first day on the job was when I met my friends Bonnie and Burn. Bonnie and Burn worked for Colsa Corporation. Burn was a computer programmer in my group, and Bonnie was in human resources. I didn't know it at the time, but they would end up having my back, and I needed it. I was green to the work world. I was battered and bruised, and the odds were stacked against me. How I made it I'll never know. They helped me, and that is all that matters now. Burn was overly curious about my injuries, but she didn't pry too much. She isn't nosy, but nothing gets past her. Like I said, Burn is the most inquisitive person I've ever known. She asked me all the questions. She didn't let up, either. Bonnie would listen and make funny little wisecracks. Bonnie has a loving quality and the funniest sense of humor. Both were loving characters, and both were knowledgeable. They had seen many aspects of life between them. They worked very hard at teaching me the ropes.

As time went by, we became great friends. We ended up having lunch together almost every day. At a minimum, we met at the water cooler to have our little gossip session. Life was anything but mundane. It was during this time that I pretended to know it all. My paranoia and "boy who blew himself up" syndrome were showing, but Bonnie and Burn didn't know that was my problem. I put up a front. They knew a twenty-eight-year-old fresh out of college had not seen much of life. Yet some sort of evidence showed that there was a hurt or need. They might have been able to see some of my disorders, but I never asked them what they saw, and they never asked me anything. If they did see something, they didn't let on. Still, they saw more than I wanted to show. How wise they were for their insight! My life was sordid to say the least.

Over time I was able to reveal more about myself, and they accepted me. They knew my work world was dysfunctional. There goes that word again. Anyway, they both knew and were still accepting. I know Bonnie had to see it; she had a bit more training. I did everything I could to keep it together during the time we worked together. It wasn't long before my grandmother got sick and my precarious finances caught up to me. I was running every night just to go to sleep.

Then one day I was with Burn in a meeting. We were all gathered around, and the subject of new television shows came up. The show *Friends* had just aired. I know, right? I am really showing my age. The meeting was about to start, and somebody mentioned Matt LeBlanc. I said, "He is so hot," without realizing I'd said it. You could have heard a pin drop. Burn tried to keep the conversation going, but even she couldn't. And if she couldn't, nobody could. Just then the leader of our group chimed his glass and called for everybody's attention. He said that we hadn't had a party in a long time and, quote, "You can bring your wives, husbands, and significant others." That was the owner's son. I have other gripes about him, but not about his open-mindedness. Burn handled it beautifully, but I knew she couldn't wait to report back to Bonnie.

Over the years, my life got harder. I looked back and wished for the good ol' days. I had a lot of learning to do, and I still think there is a lot of learning ahead. In fact, we learn until life ends. That is what life is all about. I stay in contact with Bonnie and Burn to this day, though not as much as I would like. I know that life got in the way. Mine wasn't supposed to turn a little south, but I know our friendship is solid. We will see each other again. It's just around the corner.

Most of my other friendships have been cultivated outside the work world. They are either lifelong or have been picked up along the way. I am lucky for the odd sort of way life has chosen to bring us together. We get to say that without so-and-so, I wouldn't know them. For example, my friend John was introduced to me by my late friend Scott. Tyson and Tracy were introduced to me by my brother's best friend, Rip, who has also since passed away. All of this backs up my theory that you never know how or when you will meet a new friend. My friends Gary and Daniel, who are brothers, were introduced by Lori's son Zac.

Even my friend Todd was befriended in the weirdest way. He was going to beat up my brother, and I told him that was unacceptable. I told him he would have to go through me first. We decided we would be friends instead, and his is the longest friendship I have had. He never cares about my disorders. In fact, he is very supportive. He knows about the meltdown and he was there, just like John, to help me put myself back together.

John, on the other hand, is quite the character. He is a movie buff. He keeps up with actors like they were his best friends. He remembers their roles, and when the movie is over, he looks up their credits and watches YouTube clips of them. John is also the busiest and most versatile worker bee there is, with a resume a mile long. He never ceases to incorporate a new skill, and I often wonder how we got to hanging out. I do feel intimidated by him at times. Sometimes I argue with his politics because I don't agree, and sometimes it's just to hear him mumble. He is staunch in his beliefs and my

201

opinions won't sway him, even if I show him articles I've read. It isn't that he hasn't read articles himself; I just wonder where he gets his. Oh, and CNN is the Communist News Network.

This leads me right into three wonderful people that have shaped my life in numerous ways. I am lovingly referring to Scott, Beverly, and Scott's mom Dottie. Without Dottie I would never have found the perfect place to call home. We searched for what seemed like forever. Just when I blubbered that I would never find the right place, she showed me what I affectingly call home. Speaking of home, that is where Scott can find me for what we call our fix. Mostly, we have Stakeout or go to the movies. Beverly, Scott's wife, generously shares his time with me. All three are proper and very much understand my situation. They never once let me feel less than normal.

Last but not least, the two brothers, Gary and Daniel. They are a world apart, but both stand tall in their own right. Gary has a heart of gold, and Daniel…oh, how do I say it? He has a mind that is too sharp for him to master. That is not to be construed in any negative content. Both boys were raised right, and they have made me remember what it was like to be young. I applaud them for that. Neither understands when I say, "I'm tired and too old for that," but I will admit that playing video games is a blast. I also have a world of respect for their parents, Janet and John, who accept me without knowing any of my flaws.

I want to discuss all my friendships, but it is better to discuss my disorders. I have to stay focused. My schizoaffective disorder makes me leery of strangers, not of my acquaintances. I do wonder where I stand when I meet up with them at a function. I try never to bring up anything related to my disorders. As a matter of fact, I try very hard not to bring up my life at all. I don't feel comfortable discussing anything because I feel like people always have a motive for bringing it up. I try to keep the conversation centered on them— what they're up to, what's new in their life. I might mention my writing to really close friends, but they have to be really close for me to open up about everything.

Here I go talking about being reserved when I should be discussing how wonderful my friends make me feel. I know I should be grateful for their warmth and charm, because I thrive on it. I get all sorts of energy and feel all sorts of magic. I wish I could take everybody on a retreat to the mountains and just sit by a fire. Of course, I'm living a pipe dream. My friends' schedules are so different, and most of my friends don't know one another. So dream I must. Anyway, life teaches us what friendships are about, and that we have to learn through rough times. I am starting to understand what searching for a Vivid Blue is all about. I am so lucky to have such wonderful friends with so much to offer. They fill my lungs with fresh air and my soul with joy. When I think of them, my mind becomes new again! How on earth could I ever want to take one minute back or change anything that has happened? I wouldn't.

Chapter 35. I'm Not Moving...

Given enough time, I would rewrite this book over and over. But it seemed to me the right (write) thing to do was keep at it until the words melded together exactly the way they sounded in my head. I overrode my instructor and close friends. They were telling me to just publish it already so I could move on with that chapter of my life. It just never seemed right. I needed to feel confident, and that feeling never came. What you have been given, and what I wanted you to read, isn't finished. I will always feel I can do, or should I say should have done, better.

If I were to make the book better, I might just be changing what I wanted to say. It is true. I noticed from my first copies that as time went on, the meaning of the book changed from my initial intent. It didn't change a lot, but there were changes. I added more purpose, streamlined helpful ideas, paid attention to my depression. As a matter of fact, I stopped writing when I was depressed altogether. The depressed writing wasn't what I wanted the readers to see. I did want them to understand I suffered from mental illness, mainly SABP, but I also wanted them to see that I am functional with my pills. I don't care about any of the reasons why I was being diagnosed schizoaffective. Yes, occasionally it pops in my head, but I throw those pesky little thoughts out just as fast and go on with my life. Everybody has to think about something difficult, like pain, relatives dying, or a child who is misbehaving. Sometimes, my problems are easier to let go than others' thought processes. Sometimes you just say what the heck and move right along. I should have learned that sooner. I guess I'm grateful for the lessons learned today.

I started out writing a story about my life's troubles and how I managed to overcome them. Then I realized I wrote things that looked very bad for people around me and I had to edit my book. Because of this little oversight, I chopped the book in half.

Then I had to rewrite the scenes where I had too much emotion, because I didn't want to embellish the truth. Sometimes the truth goes beyond the point of believability. I chopped out another huge portion of my book.

Also, accuracy was necessary. I needed to know that my version of reality was indeed the way it happened. I cyclically rethought everything. I guess that doesn't mean it is totally correct. Personal interpretation is always skewed, and I am schizoaffective.

Most of all I needed to write in a way that I hoped would help people understand my point of view. Wow, how do you see your baby with somebody else's eyes? I daresay that might be one ugly baby, but she is mine.

This all changed in a short span after I got close to finishing the book and got a little stage fright about putting forth my work. I also was afraid to let the world know I was schizoaffective; there are some cruel people out there.

I asked myself many questions. What would I do if somebody asked me why I considered my burns to be significant when I had no blatantly visible scars to show for it? What would I do if somebody asked me about my sexuality, and if I had to face a really close-minded individual? What would I do when any unbelieving soul asked if my mother was a true hoarder? Would I show the scars I do have, take testimony from my friends, or take pictures of my parents' house? All this seems absurd. I am just writing a book to let people know that a person can get over his problems in life and shine like anybody else.

The last thing I wanted to do was hurt my parents. My parents have been the rock to which I have held steady, hoping to never disappoint. In my opinion, I have let them down a thousand times. I told my father a year or so ago that I thought I was a disappointment to him. His response was "Did I say that? Until I say that, don't think it." It was a sign that things were all right between us. My resolve at the time was to continue to take my medication and do what I promised him. It is hard to keep a promise that looks to the outside world like you are taking advantage of your parents. I said I would stay the course and build the business, and that is what I have done. I said I would take the medication if Dad paid for it, and that is what I have done. Vivid Blue and my search have taken me in so many directions, I sometimes wonder about my true direction. I have to think about where I stand and try to do better. I haven't pulled my own weight, and yet my disorders are managed better. What is next in my search for a Vivid Blue?

Chapter 36. Lucky Me

Over fourteen years have gone by since my grandmother passed, and I am still as sad as the day it happened. It is hard to believe it has been so long. The years haven't slipped away quickly; they have lasted an eternity. I was the luckiest in the family while Grandma was alive. I was her favorite grandson (in my mind, though my brother and I do fight over that title), which means it is the hardest position to be in her absence. I constantly bring her up when my family gets together, and I am always sad on Saint Patrick's Day (her birthday).

When my brother wishes to win the lottery, I tell him it would only ruin our lives. Sometimes I think all he sees is green. In high school, when our family was the richest, I thought my favorite color was green. Grandma wasn't there, and I had a hole in my heart the size of the Grand Canyon. My grandmother would listen to all my problems, and then she would say to me, "Other than that, you don't have a thing to worry about." She would then give me the option of weeding the garden for twenty dollars or playing her a game of Scrabble for ten dollars. Which do you think I chose? She would let me use the dictionary, and she'd look over my shoulder and say, "You can do better than that."

When I didn't feel well, I used to say, "I want to lay down."

"Are you going to lay an egg?" she would ask lovingly.

"No, ma'am," I would reply, "I am going to *lie* down." She always had a wise word to say about something I did or said.

Finding love in other people is a necessity in life. There will always be people we revere. It is true, the people who have helped me have been disappearing, but it also seems that I have been helping others more and more. Through it all, there have been a lot of ups and downs. I'm grateful for the people in my past and for my past experiences. It is the vivid people who guide you in making the right choices. Their advice allows you to realize what is important.

I am trying to make a difference and pay it forward. I guess that's the way it ought to be. When you try to help, the next generation takes it and moves about in ways that seem selfish. This would be the pattern. I have come to the conclusion it's not a selfish thing. It is the way of the world. When it comes to the next generation, they have to move on and go forward with their lives. You must go on with your life. You can see a little of this generosity unfold. You pretend not to notice when they take what they need. You stay in one place and they tend to be moving. They hustle and bustle to get their lives together. Hopefully they can find happiness and peace at some point. Maybe you'll ultimately find the most pleasure in seeing their happiness manifest into their dreams. There's no sense in bragging about it, pointing it out, or jotting it down. Altruism of any kind makes you feel proud. The real reward is just knowing that people are actually the taking the recycled advice of somebody who's helped you. The reward is its own little blessing of morality and maturity.

There are so many blessings in my life that I can't list them without leaving a few out. I try not to take advantage of the good in my life. I have been lucky to have parents who have been together for over fifty-three years. It is a blessing to have my parents alive and still willing to help me. Several people in my group meetings feel they don't have any supportive family members, and that is sad. Even my brother is now supportive of my treatment, and he thinks I am on the right path. It would be neglectful if I didn't mention how lucky I am to have the greatest gift God can bestow on a human, the love of a pet. My greatest gifts outside the love of my family are my cats, Sophie and Sebastian. They have never been a disappointment or a burden (even when they have been bad!), and they give abundant joy. I know others feel that way about their pets. I won't trumpet about mine too much other than to say I am biased in every way possible. I often wonder if I deserve the gift God has granted me. Surely I must have done something right at some point in my life.

My cats' crazy antics as young kittens playing makes me think of the way we humans need to be when times get tough. We need to stop the seriousness of the situation and play. As a person suffering from schizoaffective disorder, OCD, and PTSD, this is the hardest thing for me to do. I thank God every day for my two cats.

They both take turns helping me with my disorders.

The greatest things in life are never going to be written on paper like they are lived in life. The search for my Vivid Blue manifests itself in realizing and understanding what the most important things are all about. While I don't claim to have all the answers, I do know there are things we need to make the world go around. It would be very simplistic of me to say love is the key, because that has been said so many times before. Yet we all know it to be true. I have been blessed to have wonderful friends and family to give me support. I know that I never would have made it this far without their help and concern. I don't even try to kid myself into thinking I could make it without them. I know that diet and medicine are key components to this equation, but I can't stress enough the power of a positive attitude. The ability to laugh off your mistakes is priceless when it comes to self-preservation. How you look at the future determines what kind of future you will have too.

Where I will be tomorrow isn't always going to be where I'd planned. I know I never planned to be here, and certainly not with a mental illness. I can, however, plan to be in better places. Hope is a gift God granted us when he gave us our incredible minds. Hope for tomorrow is everything a SABP person should have at the low points of his or her life. I know there are points where my hope is less than what it needs to be. I also know I need to fall back on others without the overbearing pride that tangles me in a web of conceit. I will overcome many more obstacles placed before me. I will survive.

Hope is never elusive. Hope has generously placed many things before me, and I am very grateful. My search for a Vivid Blue has illuminated most of the important ones. The search has taken me to five countries and just under half of the United States, only to find there is no better place than with family and friends. I am glad to know that after fifty years of scaring people off, the ones who stuck around are the true friends.

The Vivid Blue in my life will always be my memory of the loved ones who showed me the way. They taught me what it means to be loving and genuine. I hope they realize they were my support in writing this book. I only hope my book will help somebody.

My Vivid Blue is all about truth, honesty, perseverance,

compassion, understanding, happiness, friendship, pride, honor, support, forgiveness, and most of all love. Vivid Blue isn't a color. It is something you own. It is memories, values, and ethics that never fade. It is hopes and dreams that manifest themselves in the corners of our lives. I think this is the "prettiest blue" that my grandmother said she saw when she grabbed my arm just before she died.